JERUSALEM
REVISITED

the liturgical meaning of holy week

---

jerusalem revisited

KENNETH STEVENSON

The Pastoral Press
Washington, D.C.

Jerusalem Revisited—The Liturgy of Holy Week, being a series of lectures delivered at the College of the Resurrection, Mirfield, during Holy Week, 1984.

ISBN: 0-912405-53-8

The Pastoral Press
225 Sheridan Street, NW
Washington, DC 20011
(202) 723–1254

The Pastoral Press is the Publications Division of the National Association of Pastoral Musicians, a membership organization of musicians and clergy dedicated to fostering the art of musical liturgy.

Printed in the United States of America

CONTENTS

PREFACE

Holy Week has figured prominently in twentieth century liturgical renewal. For Roman Catholics it all really began in 1951 with the restoration of the Easter Vigil. Then came the reforms of 1956. Finally, the Missal of 1970 took these reforms even further. Moreover, my own (Anglican) Church has also taken part in the liturgical renewal of Holy Week and has made several important contributions both to the study of the history of this "Great Week" and, along with many other Christian churches of the West, has also produced revised services.

In 1984 Father Benedict Green, C.R. invited me to deliver a series of lectures on Holy Week to the students of the College of the Resurrection, Mirfield, England. It was a great privilege to live with that vigorous community for a few days and to test out some of the ideas which may now find a more expanded and permanent form in the pages which follow. Some of this material has already appeared, in considerably reduced form, in the little book written by Michael Perham and myself on the 1986 Church of England services and which was published in that year by S.P.C.K. under the title, *Waiting for the Risen Christ*.

Holy Week will continue to fascinate people because it deals with the central mystery of the Christian faith—the death and resurrection of Christ. It fascinated me as a parish priest, as a seminarian, and as a boy. I gladly dedicate this book to my parents, Eric and Margrete Stevenson, who taught me both to love the liturgy and to question it.

Epiphany 1988
Guildford, England

CHAPTER ONE

PROLOGUE

Approach

There is still always something different about travelling to Jerusalem. It remains different from any other place. There is an extra dimension, a depth discernible not just through the buildings and the sacred sites of past events but through the human situation itself. Indeed, pilgrims to the city can be so wrapped up in their own religiousness, so intent upon their past, that they miss what God may be saying through the present.[1]

RELIGION'S OWN BASIC PROBLEM is that it can serve only its own purposes, rather than God's, and thereby distort the truths which it seeks to express through worship, belief, and what we would call a Christian lifestyle. When it comes to Holy Week, two further problems raise their heads, and these we may express by the following caricatures.

The first caricature is the Dean of King's College, Cambridge, reading out the opening Bidding Prayer at the Christmas Eve Carol Service, known all over the world as a gem of traditional Anglican choral liturgy: "Beloved in Christ. Be it our care and delight . . . in heart and mind to go even unto Bethlehem." Surrounded by Gothic architecture, music, color, symbolism, we *could* look at Holy Week worship as an exercise in reassurance, that where the

---

1. Simon Barrington-Ward, *Church Missionary Society Newsletter* 460 (April 1984) 1.

1

Christian faith may pose questions which cause us to sit up, the liturgy not only does *not* ask questions, but *excludes* the possibility of even asking them. On this basis, Christian worship is above reproach, even discussion; we do what we are told to do, and we perform whatever authority enjoins on us. Just as the "house of peers" (in Private Willis' song in Act 2 of Gilbert and Sullivan's *Iolanthe*) leave their brains outside the British House of Lords before any debate or vote, so does the Christian community leave its brains outside the church building before it starts to worship.

The second caricature came to mind when I attended a meeting of the Manchester Medical Group in a large lecture-theater of the University's Faculty of Medicine. The Medical Group brings together doctors, nurses, moral philosophers, theologians—people from many different walks of life who are concerned about medical ethics. The theme of the seminar was in vitro fertilization, and because Manchester University has a Secular Charter which excludes any one religious persuasion from a position of authority in its life, the debate at the meeting was wide-ranging, frank, and at times very clinical and detailed. I am not used to those details in discussion, and I soon discovered that I didn't have a strong stomach for them either! The same is true, I suspect, for many who begin to look at Christian worship. For many different reasons, they do not have the stomach for examining the details which make up liturgy, whether these be based on historical studies or the human sciences.

And yet the two caricatures are complementary. As we go through the central events of this Great Week (as it was frequently called in antiquity), we need both the reverence of the Christmas Carol Service and the objectivity of the Medical Group, because we are at one and the same time handling sacred things and human things. Worship is both a supremely divine activity and a blatantly human one.[2] Again and again, Holy Week will take us back to

2. See, in general, Aidan Kavanagh, *On Liturgical Theology* (New York: Pueblo, 1984).

Jerusalem, built as a city that is at disunity with itself, and where the percipient pilgrim will sense weird tensions all around. Jerusalem is the city which Jesus entered on that donkey; whose temple he cleansed; whose clerisy found him too hot to handle; where he sat and supped for the last time with the inner circle; outside which he was arrested, for no apparent reason; inside which he was tried; and beyond which he was executed, buried, and, then, was raised to life. It is no surprise that it is the liturgy of Jerusalem that we are celebrating this week, partly the Jerusalem of the New Testament, partly the Jerusalem of the fourth century pilgrims, and partly the spiritual Jerusalem of the mixed traditions of Christianity which made up the service books and the piety of the faithful in the western churches. Those three ingredients are appropriate because Holy Week is so fully covered in the pages of the New Testament;[3] because it suddenly flourishes during the time of Constantine, when holy geography dictates that churches and shrines should be set up everywhere in the Holy Land where Jesus did this, that, or the other; and because we do *not* live in Jerusalem but in a different country, with a different religious temperament and a variegated religious history. Unlike the Bible, the liturgy does not have canonical status; it should change, preferably more than every four hundred years.

Origins

The classical liturgy of Lent and Holy Week, the one that emerges from the fourth century and after, encapsulates four main themes. One is that of contemplation on the passion of Christ, which is so central to the four gospels. Another is the penitence of the faithful, which from time to time has included those special penitents who seek the forgiveness of God in a particular way, whether folk

3. See, for example, Hans Ruedi-Weber, *The Cross: Tradition and Interpretation* (London: S.P.C.K., 1979).

who have offended the community and are excommunicated for a time, or those of us who seek the advice and counsel of a priest. Yet another is the fast before Easter, which has been widely interpreted; Athanasius[4] himself suggests three ways, which increase in rigor as he gets older (and, one imagines, as the liturgy he knows gets tougher). Finally, Easter is the day on which the new members of the church are baptized; from the third century onwards, perhaps earlier, there is a trend which restricts baptism to Easter and Pentecost, Easter being preferable because this is the day on which God raised Jesus, the day on which the believer spiritually dies and rises with Christ. Many of the new prayers of the 1970 Missal and many other modern service books are in fact deeply traditional in that they reflect this early tradition of Easter as the baptismal feast. For those of us who have already been baptized, this annual celebration is more than a reminder; it is a renewal, because baptism is not something which the church "does" to people, but is a mystery in which the whole church grows.

That baptismal liturgy of Easter night—the paschal liturgy—is the museum-piece of the whole week. If we are to look at things from a coldly historical perspective, then Easter night stands on its own as the "first stratum," to use the language beloved of Gregory Dix.[5] It is difficult for us to imagine just how dramatic and important was this Christian vigil, to which we shall return in a later chapter. An Easter sermon by Melito of Sardis (c. 170) has come down to us which gives us evidence of an already established celebration of the Christian Passover, with a long series of Old Testament lessons, culminating in the Easter message of the New:

4. See Thomas J. Talley, *The Origins of the Liturgical Year* (New York: Pueblo, 1986) 168ff. for a full discussion of the issues raised by the evidence.

5. Gregory Dix, *The Shape of the Liturgy* (London: Dacre, 1945) 434–527 where Dix exemplifies the theory of the "three strata" in the evolution of the eucharist.

4

Now grasp this, dearly beloved; how it is new and old, eternal and transient, corruptible and incorruptible, mortal and immortal, the mystery of the Pasch.[6]

It would never have occurred to Christians living then to have had a Holy Week at all. For them it was sufficient to celebrate the death and resurrection of Jesus in one fell swoop. No doubt the week leading up to this Passover was marked by fastings, devotions, readings of the passion, and, where appropriate, baptismal preparation. But this all-night liturgical performance was enough in itself to say it all.

"Historicism"[7]

The "second stratum" of Holy Week does not really come until the fourth century, when that phenomenon which we call "historicism" takes over. Gregory Dix was fond of driving a wedge between the early (pre-Nicene) church's *eschatological* worship and the later (post-Nicene) church's *historical* worship; fortunately, recent scholarship has questioned him. The seeds of historicism are to be found in the third century, and even on a weekly basis, for there is evidence that in some traditions Wednesday was a day for thinking about the betrayal of Christ, and Friday was a day of the crucifixion. Wednesdays and Fridays, according to the *Didache* at the end of the first century, are to be the fast days, in order to be different from the Jewish ones, Mondays and Thursdays!

This "historicism" was a result of different attitudes. Constantine undertook a policy of putting up buildings at important religious centers, and his mother's visit to dedi-

6. Translation by Thomas Halton from the French text, in A. Hamman, *The Paschal Mystery,* Alba Patristic Library 3 (Staten Island: Alba House, 1969) 26. For the Greek text see O. Perler, *Méliton de Sardes, Sur la Pâques et fragments,* Sources Chrétiennes 123 (Paris: Cerf, 1966) 60.

7. See Robert F. Taft, "Historicism Revisited," in *Beyond East and West: Problems in Liturgical Understanding* (Washington, D.C.: The Pastoral Press, 1984) 15–30.

5

cate churches at Bethlehem and around Jerusalem was long remembered by local Christians. Christianity, which had long been formalized before 325, could enjoy imperial favor. Pilgrims flocked to Jerusalem and its environs; our earliest account is by an anonymous traveller from Bordeaux in 333, just seven years after work had begun on a proper church at Golgotha, the traditional site of the crucifixion of Christ, and two years before its dedication.

As is usual at critical points in the church's history, a strong character emerges to give expression to the spirit of the age. Cyril delivers his catechetical lectures to baptismal candidates, and probably to others as well, in about 348, and deliberately strengthens the "dying and rising" (Rom 6:3–11) imagery of baptism, as opposed to the "Jordan" imagery which later preachers use, and which recent studies suggest to have been the older pattern.[8] Then later, while Cyril was bishop of Jerusalem (from c. 351), the liturgy of Holy Week takes off. We read of a Holy Week program inaugurated by Cyril which would have exhausted the most assiduous church-attender. But it clearly fascinated Egeria, the nun who visited Jerusalem between 381 and 384 and who wrote down what she witnessed. One of the human features of the Jerusalem liturgy in the next generation is how the time-table is considerably lightened under Cyril's successor!

Historicism, geography, and pilgrimage give rise to another factor in our story, what might be called the "liturgical trade-route." This is more than a general desire to make Christianity public and embedded in time and stonework, which is really the *Zeitgeist* of that fourth century. It is that curious phenomenon known to many people,

8. See Gabriele Winkler, *Das Armenische Initiationsrituale: Entwicklungsgeschichtliche und liturgievergleichende Untersuchung der Quellen des 3.bis 10.Jahrhunderts,* Orientalia Christiana Analecta 217 (Rome: Pontificium Institutum Studiorum Orientalium, 1982). Summarized in "The Original Meaning of the Prebaptismal Anointing and Its Implications. A Study of the Armenian, Syriac and Greek Terminology," *Worship* 52 (1978) 24–45.

including those not particularly interested in liturgy, whereby a certain custom is seen on its home-territory and taken somewhere else, for all kinds of reasons. It is transported from where it began into another place, and (usually) adapted. This is how the Palm procession and the veneration of the cross migrated to the West—from Jerusalem. Fascinating to the liturgist is the difference between the performance in the old country and the fusion of those customs with older practices in the new. The "trade-route" operates inevitably; you only have to think of the way the offertory procession at the eucharist spread like wild-fire among parish churches in the 1930s. And, as we all know, once a new practice on a special occasion won acceptance by the people of a given time and place, it takes more than the ingenious innovating cleric to dislodge or replace that custom. Liturgy is a conservative business, and nowhere more so than at times like Holy Week. History, geography, and the trade-route produce the pattern which is familiar to many people today. The Easter Vigil remains, as a delightful liturgical fossil, standing on its own. But the scheme works backwards from early on the Sunday morning, when that old service ends. Friday is the day of crucifixion; therefore let's have a service to celebrate it. Thursday is the day of Supper, agony, arrest, and trial; therefore let's have services to celebrate one or other of these. Monday, Tuesday, and Wednesday have various associations, mainly looking forward to these central events. The Sunday before is the day on which Jesus entered Jerusalem to the shouts of all and sundry; therefore let's celebrate that, too. In this way the classical liturgies of the West operated, taking a lead from Jerusalem, but showing remarkable vivacity in the way new ideas were absorbed and adapted, a lesson which they have a great deal to teach us, particularly where the liturgy is performed in somewhat anemic and clinical manner. For liturgy is above all an activity of the imagination, and when the church forgets that, worship becomes arid, and new practices emerge, through the back-door.

7

This is precisely what happened during the later Middle Ages. From the tenth century onwards, there grew up a trend which linked Good Friday and Easter Day in a way which the older liturgies failed to do, in rites and ceremonies surrounding the burial of Christ.[9] In many places this was linked with the consecrated host, which later on was sometimes carried in procession on Palm Sunday, as in Rouen and Sarum (Salisbury) and elsewhere. These additions, which we may call "stratum three," provided the liturgy with a dramatic quality which also matched popular piety. It has its own lessons, too, for when "drama" is incorporated into the liturgy, it runs the risk of becoming formalized, stylized, and can therefore lose its magic.

But the story is incomplete without mentioning the Reformation, where, in Anglican and Lutheran traditions, a compromise was reached. The old lections are kept and adjusted, but the ceremonies disappear; and the old vigil, which had for some time been anticipated so that it was actually celebrated on Saturday *morning*, was swept aside. This brings us to where we are today; Reformation traditions less fearful of traditional ceremonies, and a much revised Roman Catholic observance of Holy Week. But the story is really endless, and it should be so. You only have to look at the different ways in which artists have depicted the crucifixion to see evidence for the variety of religious and social experience which Christians and non-Christians bring to Calvary and its surrounding events and sequel. The re-living of these "events," however, is and must be different from the first time they happened, because we know the outcome and because we are different people every year. The final twist is the warning with which I began, that we should be ready to see what God is saying to us in the present, and therefore let the liturgy aid us in that vital quest.

9. O. B. Hardison, Jr., *Christian Rite and Christian Drama in the Middle Ages* (Baltimore: Johns Hopkins Press, 1969) 139ff.

So much for historical development. What of the pieties behind them? To try to describe piety is as slippery as a banana-skin, and yet it is sometimes necessary to attempt it. There are, in fact, three distinctive pieties,[10] modes of religious attitude, that helped to produce these rites. The first is what may be called "unitive," and it sums up all that the early, single paschal liturgy expresses. "Unitive" piety approaches the Easter mystery as a single and wholesome affair in which the faithful gather to celebrate the death and resurrection in one liturgy, through the night. For such a pristine piety there is no need to "historicize" but rather in light, word, water, and bread and wine, to pass from death to life with Christ. Such a religious experience is stark and austere, and (as we shall see) full of liturgical symbolism. But it is quite different from the next two.

The second piety is what may be called "rememorative,"[11] and it lies behind the trend toward "historicism" which we have already seen from the fourth century onwards. In rememorative liturgy certain "events" are celebrated in a vaguely historical fashion, with symbolism attached to each. This is the kind of piety Egeria entered into so fully at Jerusalem. But the use of symbolism is significant. A relic of the "true" cross is venerated on Good Friday—but there is no "re-enactment" of the events leading up to the crucifixion, nor the crucifixion itself. There are various "rememorative" services in the preceding days of the "Great Week," but no one acts parts in the play. The liturgy is allowed to find its own ambience through context of scripture reading, geographical association, and continuity. Finally, on Palm Sunday, the faithful walk down the Mount of Olives, but there is no donkey. It is these "rememorative" rites that provide the basic struc-

10. Kenneth Stevenson, "On Keeping Holy Week," *Theology* 89 (January 1986) 32ff.
11. See Hardison, *Christian Rite and Christian Drama* 141.

9

ture and ideas for the classical western liturgies that appear in the 1970 Missal, as well as many other modern service books, including the 1979 Book of Common Prayer of the Episcopal Church. "Rememorative" piety mixes best with classical liturgy.

The third piety enters by the back door,[12] for it is hard to determine exactly *when* it begins. Its basic rationale is that the liturgy is to be dramatic, and examples of it abound in the medieval era. Perhaps the later Jerusalem "burial of the *cross*" which replaced the veneration signals its appearance. Certainly the later Byzantine "burial of *Christ*" is a representational liturgy, where the *epitaphion* (a large colored silk representation of Christ being buried) dominates the Good Friday evening liturgy. In the West, the dramatic interlude in the Easter liturgies which is called the *quem queritis* ("whom do you seek") (Jn 20:15) illustrates the development eloquently. The drama first appears in England in the tenth century, and it sometimes occurs during the Paschal Vigil, with various ministers suddenly "acting" the parts of the women at the tomb, and one of them taking the part of Christ. A contemporary writer commented that its purpose was for "strengthening the faith of the unlearned common persons and neophytes."[13] (Neophytes were the newly-baptized.) But representational piety persists through the Middle Ages, and it gives rise to other customs which make the liturgy "meaningful" and "relevant."

For example, the host is "buried" in an Easter sepulcher. The priest washes the feet of the twelve "disciples" on Thursday. And a penitential air of gloom surrounds the whole week itself. But it spreads further. Devotions like the "Stations of the Cross" migrate across Europe as an

12. See note 11 above. See also Kenneth Stevenson, "The Ceremonies of Light—Their Shape and Function in the Paschal Vigil Liturgy," *Ephemerides Liturgicae* 99 (1985) 175ff. (Whole article 170–185)
13. Quotation from the *Regularis Concordia* quoted in Hardison, *Christian Rite and Christian Drama* 192.

ingenious way of re-creating Jerusalem on alien soil, at any point in the liturgical year, though usually during Lent, on an individual basis and (be it noted) easily repeatable. Thus, the individual pious person hovers before the cross in order that Christ may enter his or her heart.

It need hardly be said that such a piety paved the way for the Reformation. Some traditions (Anglican and Lutheran) deliberately kept the liturgical year, whereas assiduous followers of Zwingli and Calvin did not. But the religious experience was still cross-centered, even though all these churches rid themselves of special ceremonies of Holy Week (and at any other time of the year). Thus, Anglican and Lutheran service books excluded the palm prologue to the eucharist on the Sunday before Easter; so the palm procession and readings disappear, to reveal the older passion-theme eucharist on its own. But the piety and religious experience of many folk, both in the Catholic Counter-Reformation and the Lutheran, Reformed, and Anglican Churches, was representational, as can be seen in ordinary prayers and hymnody.

The mainstream churches of the twentieth century thus contain a residue of two millennia of liturgical practice and change. And in Holy Week the three pieties coexist. Unitive piety is austere, primitive, and, if you are liturgically patient, it likes the kind of liturgical celebration which is theologically the least demanding in *detail*. Rememorative is, as we have seen, midway, still employs subtle symbolism and requires elaboration, preparation, and (most important of all) a vibrant community in order to provide continuity and concentration. Representational, on the other hand, is the culmination of the pictorial mind, the result of popular piety, which is potentially vulgar, and which perhaps appeals more to the "cathedral" rather than the "monastic" type of spirituality.

In spite of all' that we liturgists keep saying, I suspect that in all the major churches of the West today, representational piety, with all its theological demands on the *cognoscenti*, is far more common than rememorative, even

11

though the classical liturgical rites in those churches are decked out with reformed rites that are undoubtedly re-memorative in their style and content. By contrast, the unitive piety of the Easter Vigil finds difficulty in engaging with popular piety, because it is so different; and yet, for those who find the apologetic demands of crudely repre-sentational piety too great (complete with its often obses-sive spelling out of details and "events"), the old Easter Vigil is exactly what they are looking for.[14]

Diversity, But a Common Purpose

Perhaps such a mélange of religious expectation should not surprise us, since we are all heirs of various traditions, and there has been so much liturgical reform in recent years. In the pages which follow, an attempt will be made to explain the history of the Holy Week liturgies, which will lead up to the main services of Holy Week as these are contained in the 1970 Missal. But, for obvious ecumenical reasons, the scope of our survey will not be exclusively western (nearly all the important ceremonies of the week are eastern in origin) nor exclusively Roman Catholic (other churches are heirs to tradition, too). Again and again, the liturgical trade-route will become apparent, with a ceremony starting life in Jerusalem, and then, as we have seen, migrating West, either to Rome directly or else *via* the more exotic liturgical traditions of Spain ("Visi-gothic") or France ("Gallican"). As the Middle Ages carry on their elaboration, so too does the liturgy, whether in great Romanesque buildings of the Ottonian Empire (in the tenth century Romano-Germanic Pontifical, written in Mainz c. 950) or in the later papal liturgy (in the thirteenth century Pontifical of Durandus of Mende). But just as then, so today, liturgy is constantly evolving, as much in text as in context, for, above all, it is in religious experi-ence, derived from common worship, that our own piety

14. See Stevenson's articles cited above, notes 10 and 12.

is fed, built up, and constantly matured. Liturgy exists to serve the church. Nowhere is this more true than when Christians gather to celebrate the central mysteries of salvation, in order to proclaim the wonders of him who has called us out of darkness into his own marvellous light (1 Pt 2:9).

> Christ yesterday and today,
> the beginning and the end,
> Alpha and Omega,
> all time belongs to him,
> and all ages:
> to him be glory and power,
> through every age and for ever.[15]

15. *The Sacramentary* (New York: Catholic Book Publishing Company, 1974) 172.

CHAPTER TWO

ENTRY: PALMS AND ACCEPTANCE

Eastern Origins

Jacob tied an ass to a vine-stalk and waited.
Then came Zechariah, who detached it and
  gave it to his Lord.
The prophet gave it to his Lord, and he mounted it; and
Zechariah walked before him, crying "Receive your king."

Zion said: "Why does he come? I have not called him."
The prophet said: "He is your king and he comes to reign."
Zion said: "I do not want him to reign over me."
The prophet replied: "He will reign over the Church,
  and you, he will abandon."

Zion said: "I will not open my doors to him,
  he will not enter."
The prophet replied: "The Church will open her own, and
  will receive him."
Zion said: "If he enters my walls, I will crucify him."
The prophet replied: "But his cross is living,
  and it will crush you."[1]

THIS LITTLE DIALOGUE-MEDITATION is part of a *Ba'utha*, a
special "argumentative" hymn, an example of which is
sung before the blessing of the palms in the Syrian rite

---

1. Translation of the French text in Georges Khouri-Sarkis, "La semaine sainte dans l'église syrienne," *La Maison-Dieu* 41 (1955) 97. On
the literary character of the liturgical tradition, see Sebastian Brock,
"Dialogue Hymns of the Syrian Churches," *Sobornost* 5:2 (1983) 35–45.

today. In a reflective and dramatic motif, the church brings together the Old and New Testaments and affirms the fundamental spiritual paradox of Holy Week. Palm Sunday is, in one sense, an absurd affair. Zion's mind is closed, but the prophet's is not. The church prefers her routine attitudes, but there is a voice in the wilderness ready to debunk the tradition in order to point to the world upsidedown: "But his cross is living, and it will crush you." We human beings cannot make up our mind about God; one moment we wave branches at him, and a few days later we lynch him on a common tree. The Syrian tradition, deep-rooted and native on Jerusalem soil, captures what modern jargon would term the "ambivalence" of the Great Week.

The Jerusalem services which Egeria attended reflect this, too, but in a manner which is a little unfamiliar to us. She tells us that the Sunday eucharist and other morning services amounted to doing "everything as usual," that tantalizing phrase which she uses when what Cyril does is the same back home in Spain, where Egeria probably came from. A lectionary from Jerusalem a century later tells us that the gospel reading was Matthew 20:29–21:17, the narrative of the palm entry. But her silence on this and later western tradition suggests that a passion narrative might have been read, perhaps that of Matthew.[2]

But, says Egeria, "At one o'clock all people go up to the Eleona Church on the Mount of Olives (named after Elena, Constantine's mother)" for a service which lasts until three, and from there they go to the Imbomon, the place from where Jesus is supposed to have ascended into heaven, for another service, which lasts until five. At its conclusion the palm gospel is read from Matthew. Let Egeria herself describe what follows:

2. See John Wilkinson, *Egeria's Travels* (London: S.P.C.K., 1971) 132 and 266 (Armenian Lectionary).

At this the bishop and all the people rise from their places, and start off on foot down from the summit of the Mount of Olives. All the people go before him with psalms and antiphons, all the time repeating, "Blessed is he that cometh in the name of the Lord." The babies and the ones too young to walk are carried on their parents' shoulders. Everyone is carrying branches, either palm or olive, and they accompany the bishop in the very way the people did when once they went down with the Lord. They go on foot all down the Mount to the city, and all through the city of Anastasis [main church, of the resurrection], but they have to go pretty gently on account of the older women and men among them who might be tired.[3]

Egeria's humanity and eye for detail make her readable, tender, accurate, and sometimes amusing. Why not? Liturgy is superbly funny business, especially when people fail to see the humor. One can imagine her excitement in taking part in this procession, though her comments on what she saw are so economical in their scope that we are left wondering whether she found the strain of an all-afternoon set of liturgies somewhat burdensome. Nonetheless, we are faced with an "everything as usual" series of morning offices and eucharist, followed by this afternoon sit-in and walk-about. The magic of the liturgy is the way in which this new, but perhaps obvious, custom spread and was incorporated into the older "usual" structures. How is it adapted? Returning for a moment to the Syrian rite,[4] we can note that the palm liturgy dominates the whole eucharist, but with the kind of solemn paradox which is enshrined in the hymn quoted earlier. After hymns and chants to begin the eucharist, there follows a sequence of Old Testament lessons, Genesis 49:8–12 (part of Jacob's deathbed prophecy), Zechariah 2:10–17 (the prophecy of the king coming to Jerusalem), and Isaiah

3. See note 2 above, 132.

4. See Khouri-Sarkis, "La semaine sainte" 96–99. For a comparison, see Emmanuel Lanne, "Textes et rites de la liturgie pascale dans l'ancienne église copte," *L'Orient Syrien* 6 (1961) 279–300.

52:7–9 ("how beautiful on the mountains ... "). These venerable lections, which gave rise to the chants themselves, have disappeared. At the gospel the Lucan version of the palm entry is read (Lk 19:29–40). After a special litany, the branches are blessed and distributed, and the procession begins, led by cross and tapers, with the president at the rear, surrounded by children; the route takes them out of a side door and in through the main door, and the eucharist is taken up where it left off, but with another gospel, this time the Johannine palm narrative (Jn 12:12–22).

The Syrian rite makes the palm story the dominant theme of the eucharist, with all the exuberance and symbolism which that liturgical tradition is known for; and one may hazzard a guess that Jerusalem tradition and the popularity of the procession Egeria describes gave rise to this unitive structure for the morning eucharist on the Sunday before Easter. If there was an earlier practice of reading the Matthew passion narrative, then it has long since disappeared. The Syrians have brought palms right into the heart of their eucharist; their synaxis was sufficiently flexible to open up into a procession.

But that is not the end of it. In the evening they have the Office of Lamps (*Nahire*),[5] which is celebrated in a darkened church, with all the morning's decorations removed. Behind the altar a large black panel is placed, on which are depicted a white cross surrounded by the instruments of the passion—Pilate's whip, the crown of thorns, the sponge of vinegar, among others. The office begins with prayer, and hymns and chants concerning the parable of the ten virgins; the gospel (Mt 25:1–3) is read from an ambo in the center of the church, where the ambo used to be originally; Psalm 118 (117) is chanted, during which the congregation processes together with the clergy outside the church, and stops at the main door, which is shut. The door is taken to represent the gate of heaven;

5. See Khouri-Sarkis, "La semaine sainte" 99–103.

the president kneels before it and prays to be admitted to the Kingdom; he knocks three times and is granted entrance, along with the congregation; the office ends with penitential prayers.

Once again, we see some real genius in the way the spirituality of Holy Week is interpreted. Obviously, the compilers of these venerable services sought to divide palm and penitence by mood, hence the two separate services. And yet the palm eucharist stresses the rejection of Jesus by the people; and the evening office of the *Nahire* permits the people to enter the Kingdom. The one belongs to the other. But they are kept apart because, it may have been thought, there is a limit to what one single liturgy can carry.

By contrast, however, the Byzantine rite has lost its palm procession, although the morning eucharist is on the theme of palms, with accompanying chants and suitable decoration of the church.[6] Perhaps this is an example of a law in liturgy that a new feature is either adopted, hook, line, and sinker, or it is rejected because it cannot belong. In Jerusalem itself, the procession continues as an outdoor event, for obvious reasons. Its decline in connection with the eucharist in the Byzantine liturgy may be accounted for in a number of ways, including the inability of small village churches to muster an impressive array of ministers and singers. Constantinople, however, never a place wanting to be outdone by Jerusalem (or Rome, for that matter), long involved the patriarch in an elaborate procession from one church (the Forty Martyrs) to the main church.[7]

Western Christians tend to be somewhat two-minded about the ancient churches of the East. We admire their

6. See *Byzantine Daily Worship* (Allendale: Alleluia Press, 1969) 815ff; see also texts in J. Goar, *Euchologion sive Rituale Graecorum* (Venice: Javarini, 1730) 589ff.

7. See J. Mateos, *Le Typicon de la Grande Eglise: II Le Cycle des Fêtes Mobiles*, Orientalia Christiana Analecta 166 (Rome: Pontificium Institutum Orientalium Studiorum, 1963) 64–67.

primitive characteristics, and yet we are aware of the great divide between the culture which has produced, on the one hand, the phenomenon of the medieval western church and, on the other, the churches of the Reformation. It could be objected that we have nothing to learn from the East because we are so different from them. But liturgy doesn't just evolve in an imperceptible manner, like the hand of a small watch.[8] Liturgy results from the ways in which people respond to tradition and the world in which they live. Often this induces paralysis, as happened in the Roman Catholic Church after the Council of Trent. Often it gives rise to a tug-o'-war, as is happening in many western churches today. But new roads can be taken when people decide to move in a particular direction. We are not, after all, dealing with some gigantic "unmovable mover," but with people, places, and things. Those time-honored Syrian traditions have about them a poetry and lightness which can be paralleled, in a different way, by some of the popular hymnody of the Evangelical Revival, in their genius for combining sentiment and theological reflection.[9] But the essential difference is that those hymns tend to be about individuals, whereas the experience described by Egeria and mediated through the creative forces behind the Syrian rites is anything but individualistic. It is a celebration of the whole church, warps and all.

Western Adaptation

But we must move on to the West, for that is where the most interesting accumulation develops. When the palm procession migrates through the trade-route, it meets (everywhere, it seems) an already-established custom of reading the Matthew passion narrative, which has nothing to do with palms at all. In his magisterial work on the

8. See Kavanagh, *On Liturgical Theology*, esp. 122ff.
9. See below, Chapter 4, note 7.

20

early Roman lectionaries, Walter Howard Frere notes that the epistle is invariably Philippians 2:5–11 and the gospel, Matthew 26 and 27.[10] There was a conservatism about the reading of the passion narratives in Holy Week, with Luke on Wednesday and John on Friday, and then Mark was later added on Tuesday. There can be no clearer indication that, within the provenance of the Roman liturgy, from at least the sixth century, the eucharist for the morning of the Sunday before Easter was a passion celebration. On the other hand, two factors put a cloud of uncertainty over this assumption. First, the early Roman books tend to call this day the "Sunday of Palms," and yet the earliest prayers in the Mass are all concerned with the passion. It is conceivable that people brought palms to church with them, and that these were not actually *blessed* until the palm prayers arrived from elsewhere. And yet service-titles can be notoriously difficult to relate to the prayers themselves! The second factor is that the old Spanish lections for this day were to do with palms; but these could, of course, have come from the East and replaced a now lost tradition of concentrating on the passion. In the eucharist itself, a later custom arises of reading the passion narrative dramatically. The thirteenth century Salisbury rite has a bass voice for the words of Christ, a tenor voice for the narrator, and an alto voice for anyone else. This is also how the 1570 Missal directs it to be read. Earlier practice varied, but tended to have three deacons chanting in normal tone, taking those three "parts."

But what of the palm theme? It is a moot point as to when it first appears in the Roman liturgy. Evidence suggests that it came to Rome from France, for the prayer which blesses the palms seems to have been added to the best manuscripts of the Gregorian Sacramentary, yet it appears in the Gelasian books. ("Gregorian" means prop-

10. See W. H. Frere, *Studies in Early Roman Liturgy: III The Roman Epistle-Lectionary*, Alcuin Club Collections 32 (London: Milford, 1935) 8; and W. H. Frere, *Studies in Early Roman Liturgy: II The Roman Lectionary*, Alcuin Club Collections 30 (London: Milford, 1934) 38.

erly Roman, from the seventh century; "Gelasian" means "Roman-Frankish," from the seventh and eighth centuries.) But this is a matter of simply blessing palms for distribution. The old Spanish rite is probably the first of the western liturgies to dramatize the palm ceremonies; for it starts the liturgy in another church, blesses and distributes the palms, and then processes to the main church.[11] This sounds remarkably similar to the old Constantinopolitan rite, which should hardly surprise us in view of the inter-change between Spain and the Eastern Empire in the sixth and seventh centuries. On the other hand, the Spanish custom is also urban in its character, and two adjacent churches would probably have required simplification in a small liturgical milieu. When we look for "norms," they are often as much to do with local setting for the liturgy as they are concerned with which liturgical family is under discussion. The procession, however, starts life as a straightforward blessing of palms *before* the Mass; there is no question of incorporating the new ceremony into the body of the eucharist itself. The blessing-prayer, which usually combines both blessing the *branches* and praying that they may *protect* the faithful in the future,[12] gives rise to additional features, such as exorcisms, a longer blessing preceded by "Lift up your hearts," hymns during the procession, including Theodulf of Orleans' famous "All glory laud and honor" in the ninth century,[13] and the reading of the narrative of the entry of Jesus himself into Jerusalem.

In the tenth century the Romano-Germanic Pontifical, a liturgical book which fuses Roman material with older French-German material, provides an elaborate pre-Mass

11. See *Missale Mixtum* in Migne, *Patrologia Latina* 85, coll. 338ff. See also John W. Tyrer, *Historical Survey of Holy Week—Its Services and Ceremonial*, Alcuin Club Collections 29 (London: Milford, 1932) 55ff.

12. See H. Schmidt, *Hebdomada Sancta: II Fontes Historici, Commentarius Historicus* (Rome: Herder, 1957) 693–705.

13. See Schmidt, *Hebdomada Sancta* II 653–658.

palm rite.[14] There are no fewer than four readings, which are followed by a sermon. The palms are blessed with a lengthy preface-type prayer. The procession moves round the church, an easy affair in one of those large Romanesque basilicas on the Rhine. The gospel book was customarily carried at the head of these processions. But as the Middle Ages wore on, there grew up the practice of carrying the host in this procession, popular in some of the English service books, although the Sarum one shows signs of the host's sudden arrival in the procession as something resembling a liturgical afterthought! The procession is well underway when a group of ministers appear from nowhere, carrying the sacred species into the main procession, rather like a small train joining a large one while both are going a full speed. What had begun as a dramatic re-enactment of the entry to Jerusalem, involving the whole assembly, has now developed into a complex series of ceremonies which accumulate in such a manner as to exclude the "popular" element in the service. The "schola" takes over the singing, and, where the church is monastic, the monks dominate the procession.

Obviously, this western palm procession varies from place to place. But the underlying characteristic is clear; the extra "palm service" has been prefixed to the older Mass and has accumulated extra ceremonies in order to make a focal point of the palms themselves. But I have used the word "palm" indiscriminately. In England the most common branch used on this day was willow, although box was known in many places as well.[15] The cur-

14. For a full text of the Holy Week rites in the Romano-Germanic Pontifical, see M. Andrieu, *Les Ordines Romani du haut moyen-âge I Les manuscrits*, Spicilegium Sacrum Lovaniense 11 (Louvain: University Press, 1931) 526–548. Texts also in Schmidt, *Hebdomada Sancta* II 561–601. See also Edmund Bishop, "Holy Week Rites of Sarum, Hereford and Rouen Compared," in *Liturgica Historica* (Oxford, 1918) 279–294.

15. See Tyrer, *Historical Survey of Holy Week* 55. See also, for example, the various provisions in the prayers in the local Scandinavian service books as studied by Bengt Strömberg, *The Manual from Bystorp*, Biblioteca Liturgica Danica, Series Latina II (Egtved, 1982) 24f.

rent practice of handing out tiny relics of tired Mediterranean palm is yet one more example of liturgical minimalism, no doubt compensated for by verbose "explanations" on the part of liturgical presidents. "Branches" appear as options in several medieval prayers, especially in northern Europe, where to import Mediterranean "palms" would clearly have been nonsensical. Here is one important aspect of acculturation, for the palm-cross, a relatively recent invention, is by its nature interpretative because it spells out the symbolism of Palm Sunday in linking the palm procession with the passion gospel. Similarly, those who are tempted to introduce donkeys into the liturgy on this day fail to realize that for Jesus to enter Jerusalem from the Mount of Olives riding on a donkey was the equivalent of taking a taxicab today.

Modern Reforms

The 1570 Missal provided an amalgam of medieval features: two readings before the collect and preface-type blessing; four collects; the blessing itself; and the procession. But in 1956 when the liturgical reforms began under Pope Pius XII, this elaborate scheme was much simplified.[16] The 1970 Missal goes even further, and provides two forms for the palm procession, one solemn, one simple.[17] This is in line with contemporary demands for liturgical books which officially encourage adaptation to local circumstances. Beginning with a sample introduction, there follows a prayer over the palms, and two texts are provided. The first alternative is a simple blessing, based on a traditional form; and the second avoids actually "blessing" the palms, but prays for the congregation, and its text comes from one of the many prayers for this occa-

16. See H. Schmidt, *Hebdomada Sancta: I Contemporanei Textus Liturgici, Documenta Piana et Bibliographia* (Rome: Herder, 1956) 35–42 (parallel texts of the 1956 *Ordo* and the 1954 *Missale Romanum* which it superseded).
17. *The Sacramentary* 122–125.

sion in the Romano-Germanic Pontifical. The same sensitivity about "blessing" palms is apparent in prayers for this day in other western churches, including the Anglican. In both the palm rite and the eucharist, the new three-year lectionary provides synoptic accounts of the events concerned, although the Johannine narrative of the palm entry is an alternative to Mark in year two. Modern reform has enriched us with alternatives, but at a stroke has dealt a blow to the traditional reading of Matthew's passion on Palm Sunday and John on Good Friday which persisted through the Reformation to Lutheran rites, as witness the two great Bach Passions. John remains on Good Friday, and the synoptic lections on Palm Sunday have relieved the weekdays of Holy Week itself, so that scriptural reflection can be wider and, perhaps, deeper.

At the eucharist on Palm Sunday the 1970 Missal directs that the gospel be read in traditional austerity, without incense, lights, or response. And whereas in late medieval times and in the 1570 Missal it was customary to mark the two different moods of the day by wearing red vestments for the procession and purple for the Mass, the new Missal directs only one color, and that is red. Perhaps the impact of this custom could be increased if special "passion-tide" red vestments were worn on this day and also on Good Friday, as joyous Pentecost clothing is hardly appropriate.[18]

Broadly speaking, the other main churches of the West follow this methodology of a pre-Mass palm ceremony followed by a eucharist in which a passion narrative is read. Drama is expected in both the procession itself and in the passion reading. Thus, the American Episcopal Book of Common Prayer follows a simplified Roman pattern, but with a preface form which is worth quoting in full, since it has a richness about it which is lacking in the Roman form:

18. W. St. John Hope, E. G. Cuthbert Atchley, *English Liturgical Colors* (London: S.P.C.K., 1918) 85. Some thought should be given to differentiating these two distinct uses of liturgical red.

It is right to praise you, Almighty God, for the acts of love by which you have redeemed us through your Son Jesus Christ our Lord. On this day he entered the holy city of Jerusalem in triumph, and was proclaimed as King of Kings by those who spread their garments and branches of palm along his way. Let these branches be for us signs of his victory, and grant that we who bear them in his name may ever hail him as our King, and follow him in the way that leads to eternal life; who lives and reigns . . . [19]

A marked feature of Anglican and Lutheran rites of this century is that Palm Sunday and the Holy Week liturgies are now becoming officially authorized, and are no longer regarded as the preserve of a High Church minority. So the western synthesis continues, combining palm and passion. Perhaps this theme of ambivalence is best expressed in the title for the day as it appears in the 1970 Missal: *Dominica in palmis de passione domini* means "Palm Sunday of the Passion of the Lord."[20]

So much of good liturgy is adaptation, as well as entirely fresh composition. A good example of the former is the preface in the eucharistic prayer for Palm Sunday in the 1970 Roman Missal. The compilers were faced with a number of choices. In the end, they found a fine but somewhat prolix preface embedded in that interminable document, the Supplement, written to accompany the Gregorian Sacramentary as it made itself accepted in Charlemagne's Frankish Empire at the start of the ninth century. What did they do? They pruned it; and this is how it runs:

Father, all-powerful and ever-living God,
we do well always and everywhere to give you thanks
through Jesus Christ our Lord.

19. *The Book of Common Prayer* (New York: Seabury, 1979) 271. See also Marion Hatchett, *Commentary on the American Prayer Book* (New York: Seabury, 1980) 226. Compare similar treatment in *The Lutheran Book of Worship* (Minister's Desk Edition) (Minneapolis: Augsburg Publishing House, 1978) 135.
20. *Missale Romanum* (Typis Polyglottis Vaticanis, 1970) 224.

Though he was sinless, he suffered willingly for sinners.
Though innocent, he accepted death to save the guilty.
By his dying he has destroyed our sins.
By his rising he has raised us up to holiness of life.

We praise you, Lord, with all the angels
in their song of joy.[21]

In March 1982 my father and I visited Jerusalem for the first time. It was a way of celebrating his retirement. To visit the Holy Land is to be caught in the tension between the extremes of religion and the continued suppressed and expressed racial violence that seems to be the sad lot of the supposed City of Peace. On the first morning we went to collect the car which we were to hire for that memorable week. Driving down the hill past the Jaffa gate, I suddenly saw an Arab, walking beside his camel. Only a day before, I had been back in Manchester, trying hard to finish all the things which chaplains are supposed to get done by the end of the term. There was something somewhat eerie in the experience, as I swerved the car out of the way, only just remembering that everyone was driving on what seemed to be the wrong side of the road. Then we drove down the hill and up the Mount of Olives to visit the Imbomon, complete with its footprint of the just-about-to-be-ascended Lord. We walked away, having done our duty, but not deeply impressed. Just before we got to the car, another Arab was standing proudly beside his camel. He quickly identified us. "Fathers," he said, "would you like to ride on my camel?" But I think he already realized our lack of enthusiasm. I am too accident-prone to risk sitting on one of those beasts.

"Do you want to ride?" Driving back down the Mount of Olives, there was a strange feeling of reality about the request. How ridiculous I would have felt, camel or don-

21. *The Sacramentary* 411. For sources, see A. Dumas, "Les sources du nouveau missel romain," *Notitiae* 60 (1971) 46.

key, had I ridden down that hill. Sometimes liturgy and life impinge on one another in ways that words cannot express. Perhaps that's why symbols are so fundamental to what we come together to celebrate.

CHAPTER THREE

RETURN: SUPPER AND BETRAYAL

"Receive Me Today . . . "

At your mystical supper, Son of God,
receive me today as a partaker,
for I will not betray the sacrament to your enemies,
nor give you a kiss like Judas,
but like the thief I confess you:
remember me Lord in your kingdom.[1]

THE "GREAT AND HOLY THURSDAY," as it is called in the
Byzantine rite, provides us with this little hymn as the
chant to be used both during the Great Entrance, at the
communion and at the dismissal. It is supremely appropriate for the day, as it speaks humanly and penitently of the
aspirations of the faithful in approaching the holy table
on this special occasion. Christians do not come to the
altar on this Thursday as if the occasion stands on its own.
Just as those who greet the Lord on Palm Sunday with
"Hosanna" know that "Crucify him" is to be the louder
cry later in the week, so on Thursday those who draw
near with faith pray that they will be received into the
Kingdom. The attitude is that of the penitent thief, who
confesses his wickedness, not that of the betrayer, poor

1. Translation in Robert F. Taft, *The Great Entrance: A History of the
Transfer of Gifts and Other Pre-Anaphoral Rites of the Liturgy of St. John
Chrysostom,* Orientalia Christiana Analecta 200 (Rome: Pontificium In-
stitutum Orientalium Studiorum, 1975) 54.

Judas Iscariot. Perhaps there is even a hint of the "discipline of the secret" in the words "I will not betray the sacrament to your enemies," for early Christians had to take care not to publish the details of their religion to those who would be happy to throw them to the lions.

The hymn (*troparion*) has an interesting history.[2] In the tenth century *Typicon*, or description of services, of the Great Church in Constantinople, it is directed to be sung as it is today, at no fewer than three significant points during the celebration of the eucharist; this is unique in the Byzantine rite. But evidence suggests that the hymn is older still, and that it was originally composed for use exclusively during the communion; it was certainly in use in the sixth century. And Jerusalem got it from Constantinople around the eleventh century when Jerusalem was "recovered" by the Greeks. Another peculiarity of the hymn is that it is not made up of psalm material but, like the Easter Day communion chant, is a collection of reflective verses, carrying devotional and theological ideas fitting for the day. That in itself is a warning that the Bible was not sufficient to provide the right kind of material in an undiluted form. Thursday and Easter Day require special treatment. As happens with devotional material, it eventually becomes appropriated into the main body of the liturgy, for from the fourteenth century it helps to make up a lengthy prayer said by priest and deacon before the communion at every celebration of the eucharist.[3] Liturgy sometimes has this genius for giving new uses to special material.

But we have not quite arrived at Thursday yet. It is not possible to jump from palms to supper as if there were nothing in between. Down the ages, Monday and Tues-

---

2. See Thomas H. Schattauer, "The Koinonicon of the Byzantine Liturgy: An Historical Study," *Orientalia Christiana Periodica* 49 (1983) 109ff.

3. See C. Kucharek, *The Byzantine-Slav Liturgy of St. John Chrysostom* (Allendale: Alleluia Press, 1971) 689ff.

day and Wednesday have been variously used. Egeria describes the days in some detail.[4] Monday has a special service in the afternoon, starting at three o'clock. She does not tell us which lessons are read, but the lectionary from the next century suggests Matthew 20:17–28, the story of the mother of the sons of Zebedee, which ends with the stern warning by Jesus of the cost of the Kingdom. On Tuesday there is a special service late at night in the Anastasis or main church which concludes with the long reading of Matthew's farewell discourse (Mt 24:1–26:2). This ends with the flat statement that the Son of Man is to be handed over to be crucified. Wednesday concludes even more dramatically with the bishop going into the cave of the Anastasis where Christ is supposed to have been buried, while a presbyter reads a narrative of the betrayal of Jesus (Mt 26:3–16), and Egeria adds: "The people groan and lament at this reading in a way that would make you weep to hear them."

There does not seem to have been a daily eucharist on these three important preparatory occasions. Even in the Latin West these do not appear until the sixth and seventh centuries, at a time when weekday Masses began to multiply.[5] Old traditions in Milan, Spain, and elsewhere point to lengthy Old Testament lections at the offices; in Ambrose's time the whole of Job was read on Monday, and Jonah, a less demanding experience, was read on Tuesday. Patristic Mass lectionaries contain Old Testament readings, which we may take to be a sign of antiquity. But there are other features in these days which set them apart as a sort of limbo before the end; no bell-ringing (some would regard this as a blessed relief), no elaborate music, feasts transferred not to get in the way, long extra readings at the offices, and Sarum has the Office for the Dead recited on Tuesday, with a Mass for the dead the next morn-

4. See Wilkinson, *Egeria's Travels* 133ff., 266.
5. See Schmidt, *Hebdomada Sancta* II 673–677; Tyrer, *Historical Survey of Holy Week* 71–78.

ing. Looking at these provisions, one is struck by the need to do something, but people are not quite sure what, except that the betrayal theme is an obvious one for the Wednesday, so that the stage is set for the next day. But there is nothing like the kind of uniformity of intent which we noticed in relation to Palm Sunday.

As we have already seen, the old Roman gospel readings consisted of the passion narrative: Matthew on Sunday, Mark on Tuesday, Luke on Wednesday, and John on Friday; Monday neatly gets the story of the anointing of Jesus at Bethany (Jn 12:1–9). The new lectionary (from the 1970 Missal) provides an interesting compendium.[6] There are no epistles, but readings from the servant songs of Isaiah, a happy blend of some old lectionaries as well as a nod to biblical scholarship. For the gospel, the passion narratives have disappeared, since the synoptics are now alternatives, in a three year cycle, on Palm Sunday, and John remains on Good Friday. Instead, a clever scheme is built up. Monday keeps the anointing at Bethany, but Tuesday has the prophecy of Jesus that Peter will deny him (Jn 13:21–33, 36–38); and Wednesday now has the narrative of the betrayal (Mt 26:14–25).

By contrast the British and ecumenical Joint Liturgical Group in 1971 produced a series of thematic offices, which can be used as ecumenical services, and which can also be celebrated with a eucharist.[7] Monday's theme is penitence and has the Ten Commandments with a special confession and litany, which leads into a word service, and a concluding prayer if there is no eucharist. Tuesday centers round obedience and includes the Methodist Covenant rite, which is usually celebrated in Methodist churches on a Sunday near the beginning of the calendar year. Wednesday's theme is service. The 1983 revision of these

6. *Ordo Lectionum Missae* (editio typica) (Typis Polyglottis Vaticanis, 1969) 120.
7. See *Holy Week by the Joint Liturgical Group* (London: S.P.C.K./Epworth, 1971) 21–28 and *Holy Week Services, Joint Liturgical Group* (London: S.P.C.K., 1983) 29–51.

services provides alternatives to these themes as well as enrichments to the 1971 rites: thus Monday can be a "Day of Cleansing," Tuesday a "Day of Teaching," and Wednesday a "Day of Waiting." Offices like these have the knack of getting people together for a special service at a time when in some traditions daily worship is not normal. They are also flexible in the way they can be adapted to suit local circumstances. I wonder how appropriate is the Covenant Service, tucked away on that Tuesday, whereas Methodists have traditionally kept it for another occasion on which it can be solemnly celebrated, interpreted by some of those fine Wesley hymns.[8] Interestingly, the compilers insert a baptismal creed after the old words of the covenant, "I am no longer my own, but yours." This really is a bold attempt to link the covenant with baptism; and yet covenant-renewal in the Methodist tradition is a wider concept than baptism, and is intended to focus in a completely new way on the whole of the Christian life, like a spotlight from an unusual angle which suddenly lights up baptism, eucharist, service, fellowship, word, preaching, and praise—all those rich spiritual qualities which make up the complex and authentic tradition called Methodism.

The covenant prayer, however, also illuminates Holy Week:

I am no longer my own, but yours. Put me
   to what you will,
rank me with whom you will; put me to doing,
   put me to suffering;
let me be employed for you or laid aside for you,
   exalted for you
or brought low for you; let me be full, let me be empty;
let me have all things, let me have nothing;
   I freely and wholeheartedly
yield all things to your pleasure and disposal.

---

8. On the history of this rite, see David H. Tripp, *The Renewal of the Covenant in the Methodist Tradition* (London: Epworth, 1969).

And now, glorious and blessed God, Father,
  Son and Holy Spirit,
you are mine and I am yours. So be it.
And the covenant which I have made on earth,
let it be ratified in heaven.[9]

The first time I recited those words, in a freezing chapel
in Lincolnshire, I found in them a quaint strangeness, in
the biblical echoes behind those contrasting phrases, as
well as in an Augustinian sense of dependence upon God.
Methodists are themselves ambivalent about the Covenant rite: some love it, but will only use it once a year
because, they say, it is too solemn for frequent use; on the
other hand, there are Methodists who regard the whole
thing as mumbo-jumbo, and I have even heard it described, disparagingly, as "almost Anglo-Catholic"! But
the covenant is the right note to strike at this stage in our
enjoyment of Holy Week, particularly when our focus
naturally falls on the day when the new covenant was
inaugurated.

Egeria

For us, there is a natural association of Thursday with
the Last Supper. That makes it difficult for us to realize
that to early Christians, even at the time of Egeria,[10] to link
Thursday exclusively with the institution of the eucharist
was something strange. Egeria's account of the day is
lengthy by comparison with the other days; she does refer
to what seem to be two eucharists, in the afternoon, and
she notes that at the second celebration "everyone re-
ceives Communion." But it is abundantly obvious that her
priorities lie with the lengthy evening program, and she
even notes that after the eucharist "everybody hurries
home for a meal, so that, as soon as they have finished it,

9. *The Methodist Service Book* (London: Methodist Publishing House,
1975) D.10.
10. See Wilkinson, *Egeria's Travels* 134.

they can go to the church on Eleona which contains the cave which on this very day the Lord visited with the apostles." Recent scholarship is helping us face head-on this apparent gap in procedure, for there is no evidence whatever to suggest that the fourth century Jerusalem church attempted to link the place of the Last Supper with the very mobile urban liturgy as it evolved in that crucial time.[11] A suggestion has been made giving a perceptive reason: that Christians of that time regarded the whole of the Triduum as still embodying the entire Pasch. Just as we tend to look at initiation rites of the time as if they contained the first anointing here, the baptism there, the second anointing (which, of course, is confirmation) there, so we can read Egeria's narrative in a severely episodic fashion, locking God up in little chunks of liturgical celebration. Perhaps Cyril of Jerusalem's insistence that "worship is indivisible" answers the more fundamental question, which also answers the spiritual need of Christians to avoid domesticating Christ into a series of domestic pets which require different feeding- and brushing-hours by us as we attend to them in somewhat clockwork manner. What strikes Egeria as significant about this day is that the community gathers for this long evening service which seems to last all night and consists of hymns and readings. It starts at the Eleona, but at midnight it moves up to Imbomon, the place of the ascension. At cockcrow, probably about 3:00 a.m., the service moves on "to the place where the Lord prayed," where the gospel narrative of Jesus' watch in prayer (Lk 22:41ff.) is read. Another move takes them to a nearby church, where Jesus' command to the disciples that they watch and pray (Mt 26:31–56) is read. The remainder of the account is worth quoting in full:

11. See John F. Baldovin, *The Urban Character of Christian Worship: The Origins, Development and Meaning of Stational Liturgy*, Orientalia Christiana Analecta 228 (Rome: Pontificium Institutum Studiorum Orientalium, 1987) 87ff.

From there all of them, including the smallest children, now go down with singing and conduct the bishop to Gethsemane. There are a great many people and they have been crowded together, tired by their vigil, and weakened by their daily fasting—and they have had a very big hill to come down—so they go very slowly on their way to Gethsemane. So that they can all see, they are provided with hundreds of church candles. When everyone arrives at Gethsemane, they have an appropriate prayer, a hymn, and then a reading from the Gospel about the Lord's arrest. By the time it has been read everyone is groaning and lamenting and weeping so loud that people even across in the city can probably hear it all.[12]

Egeria notes the length of the series of services, as well as the readings, and the fact that whole families took part in it all. But it is clear that it is the evening liturgies that fire her attention. Even if we were to say that she was used to a Thursday eucharist back home in Spain, she would surely have laid great stress on its historical and geographical context had the Jerusalem church made much of it. The evidence continues for a eucharist on this day: Augustine speaks of a celebration both in the morning and in the late afternoon, and he notes the difficulties concerning the latter over the question of fasting. The real clue for the later West lies in a fifth century text, the "Life of Sylvester," who was pope from 314–335, which tells us of a eucharist to commemorate the Last Supper, and also says that on this day the chrism is blessed and penitents are reconciled to the church.[13]

Two Relics

Later customs reveal this Holy Thursday to be a bit of jumble of ideas and associations. But there are two inter-

12. See Wilkinson, *Egeria's Travels* 135ff.
13. Text quoted in Schmidt, *Hebdomada Sancta* II 714, from B. Mombitius, *Sanctuarium seu Vitae Sanctorum* II (Paris, 1910) 509–510.

esting relics which show how the notion of the Christian Pasch ("Passover") survived into later antiquity and beyond.

One is in the Syrian Church, which to this day still calls this Thursday the "Pasch."[14] Continuity between the days at the end of Holy Week was the concern of many preachers, which perhaps explains the notion of the "Triduum" (= "Three Days"), which in the 1970 Missal is supposed to begin with the evening Mass on Holy Thursday. It is called the *Sacrum Triduum Paschale* (the "Three Sacred Paschal Days").[15] For those of us who are tempted to look somewhat episodically at the central events of salvation, here is one more reminder that we are not watching a television series, but growing into a great and wonderful mystery, which is all about the same God, whom Jesus comes to show us, that we may become more like him, and be equipped for the service of his Kingdom.

The second "relic" lies in the origin of a central feature of the Holy Thursday Last Supper eucharist—the foot washing. Although the *mandatum* ("command"—hence the English usage "Maundy Thursday") became, as we shall see, a significant part of medieval liturgy on this day, the reasons for its origin are not wholly clear, and it appears that the practice did not just arise out of a desire to carry out the drama of the foot washing (Jn 13). To the contrary, foot washing was part of the baptismal liturgy on Easter Eve in certain places in the early medieval West. Chromatius found it before baptism in Aquilea, and Ambrose (also late fourth century) inherited it in Milan, where it was, by contrast, practiced just *after* baptism. Moreover, Ambrose obviously was aware of how significant this difference was in so central a liturgy as the baptism during the Paschal Vigil that he felt the need to defend its use

14. *Breviarium juxta Ritum Ecclesiae Antiochenae Syrorum, Pars Verna Secunda* V (in Syriac) (Mosul, 1892) 140. See Khouri-Sarkis, "La semaine sainte" 104ff. and noted by Taft, "Historicism Revisited" 23.

15. *Missale Romanum* 243; noted by Patrick Regan, "The Three Days and the Forty Days," *Worship* 54 (1980) 17.

because Rome did not perform the practice. Augustine found it at Hippo, on Holy Thursday, but it seems that, while he washed the feet of those who were to receive baptism at the Easter liturgy, other members of the congregation were permitted to come forward and have their feet washed also. Two strands of exegesis dominate the foot washing narrative. One is to see Christ as the giver of salvation, the traditional baptismal motif; another is to see Christ as the example of humility, from which the later custom of foot washing developed.[16] Both emphases belong together in this acted parable which has as much to do with salvation and humility as it has to do with mission. But it is the *exemplum humilitatis* theme which takes over in the later liturgies.

Holy Thursday—Three Associations

It is now necessary to look at Holy Thursday in order to see how three quite separate associations grew together, in order to make up what happens today. The first concerns the reconciliation of penitents; before Vatican II this was long regarded as a liturgical fossil, and it has since been superseded by new rites of penance. The second concerns the blessing of oils, which has now been turned into a new rite, with a new theme. The third is the Last Supper eucharist, which has its own character and is the principal service for this day, especially since this eucharist was directed in 1956 to take place in the evening, and the foot washing was, also in 1956, brought right into the heart of the liturgy, instead of being, as before, an optional appendage.

16. For a full discussion of this disputed area, see Pier Franco Beatrice, *La lavanda dei piedi: Contributo alla storia della antiche liturgie cristiane,* Bibliotheca Ephemerides Liturgicae "Subsidia" 28 (Rome: Edizioni Liturgiche, 1983) 85ff. for Chromatius; 141ff. for Augustine.

Penitents

In Denmark this day is still called *Skaertorsdag*,[17] a delightful combination of the pagan "Tor," the god of thunder (producing our "Thur") and the Christian "skaer," meaning "shrive" (producing the old English "shere"). Sometimes these old names betray a conservatism of folk memories. Lent had long been a time of fasting and penitence, but there was some doubt about exactly when the penitents were to be reconciled with the church, or, as we would say in using later sacramental theology, given absolution. Innocent I in his letter to Decentius of Gubbio (a welter of liturgical procedure is contained in this correspondence dating from 416) declares that "if no illness intervenes, the custom of the Roman Church proves that they are to be absolved on the Thursday before Easter."[18] It is probable that Decentius knew of the custom of doing so on Good Friday in Milan, as Ambrose tells us. The first full liturgy we know is in the Gelasian Sacramentary, which provides three Masses for Maundy Thursday: one for penitents, one for chrism (in the cathedral), and one for the Last Supper. It is probably true that the Gelasian book is here reflecting some French features in such an elaborate provision, since the Gregorian Sacramentary tradition has only one Mass, that of the Supper.

The penitents come forward before the offertory from the place reserved for them at the back of the church and the deacon then prays to the bishop on their behalf. The bishop warns the penitents not to repeat their sins. Three prayers follow, two collects and a lengthy precatory abso-

17. See Tyrer, *Historical Survey of Holy Week* 79–81. For the Danish title see *Den Danske Salmebog* (København: Haase, 1953) 100. The Old Scots "Skire Thursday" is obviously a derivative from Norse terminology; see David D. Murison, "The Vocabulary of the Kirk," *Liturgical Review* 4 (1974) 46.

18. R. Cabié, *La lettre du pape Innocent Ier à Decentius de Gubbio (19 mars 416)*, Bibliothèque de la Revue d'Histoire Ecclésiastique 58 (Louvain, 1973) 28ff.

lution; there is also a prayer for the penitents after the communion. It is interesting that subsequent practice elaborates this simple scheme. In the Pontifical of Egbert of York, reflecting eighth century use in England, a special declaratory absolution is added, no doubt indicating how penitents of the time preferred to be absolved!

> We absolve you, in the stead of blessed Peter, the chief of the Apostles, to whom the Lord gave the power of binding and loosing. But, so far as accusation of conscience belongs to you, and forgiveness belongs to us, may God Almighty be your life and salvation and the Pardoner of all your sins.[19]

Behind those words lies, perhaps, a little self-consciousness about who pardons and how pardon is appropriated by the penitent, those two problems of theology and spirituality with which liturgy has to grapple continually.

Later books continue to restrict the presidency of this liturgy to the bishop, which has ancient warrant in canon three of the Second Council of Carthage (390): "a presbyter may not reconcile any one at a public Mass."[20] One is left to ask when this Mass outlived its practical usefulness, since the full-blown episcopal rites of the later English service books appear to be relics rather than pastoral offices which matched people's real needs. I would suggest that the increasing practice of private confession to a priest on a regular basis dislodged the older corporate liturgy as far as ordinary people were concerned; and that places us somewhere in the ninth and tenth centuries. The older Roman Pontifical still contained a form of the rite, but it was hardly ever celebrated, and there has been no great enthusiasm to revive it since the Second Vatican Council, particularly as the concern today is to give regular "private confession" a corporate and public and more liturgical set-

19. Translated by Tyrer, *Historical Survey of Holy Week* 88 n.1. Text in W. Greenwell, *The Pontifical of Egbert*, Surtees Society 27 (1853) 124.
20. Quoted from Tyrer, *Historical Survey of Holy Week* 91.

ting. The conclusion to this little part of the story, however, is that the reconciliation of penitents before Easter is a functional rather than a symbolic liturgical act: the church reconciles penitents so that they may celebrate Easter as fully part of the community once more, and for this reason I suggest that the earliest practice was not to hold a eucharist at all in connection with the rite, but to wait for the eucharist until Easter itself.

Oil

Here is another functional adjunct to Holy Week, and one which has grown considerably in popularity over the years. We known that oil was used in the liturgy of baptism from at least the early third century.[21] Hippolytus (215) and Cyprian (255) tell us that the oils at baptism (exorcism and chrism) were blessed, though it is not entirely clear how and when they were blessed; Cyprian refers to oil "hallowed on the altar." It is probable that the concept of a special eucharist for blessing the oil on this day is a fifth century innovation. And the idea of throwing in the oil for the sick (why not, while you're blessing oil anyway?) is something which the Gelasian books in their customary all-embracing fashion direct in the fullest way. It has always been restricted to the bishop; even in the East, where there is no eucharist, the chrism must be blessed by the metropolitan although presbyters can bless the other two types of oil.

The later Masses are complex indeed,[22] but the basic principles are nonetheless clear. Whereas the oil of exorcism and the chrism were originally mixed and prepared in church, people seem to have brought with them their own oil for the sick themselves, and this latter was blessed

21. See Eric Segelberg, "The Benedictio Olei in the Apostolic Tradition of Hippolytus," *Oriens Christianus* 48 (1964) 268–281.
22. See discussion, with charts, by Schmidt, *Hebdomada Sancta* II 715ff.

in a special prayer before the end of the eucharistic prayer. The two initiatory oils were blessed after communion, the various medieval books providing rich forms of prayer and blessing over them; the chrism comes first, followed by the oil of exorcism. But sometimes the order is different: the Gelasian books bless the two initiatory oils *before*, not after, communion, and, logically enough, bless the oil of exorcism before the chrism, and this order occurs in some later medieval books as well. The old Roman Pontifical kept to the other practice, namely, of blessing the chrism before the oil of exorcism, and doing both after communion. This is the order to be found in the simplified rite of the revised Roman liturgy.

Another conservative tendency lies in the survival of the practice of concelebration, which caused Amalar of Metz to comment upon in the ninth century. Concelebration certainly made the Chrism Mass a special occasion before the Second Vatican Council, although it was not really fully understood.[23]

An entirely new feature appears in the Chrism Mass of the 1970 Missal.[24] This is called *renovatio promissionum sacerdotalium*, the renewal of priestly vows. The 1970 book keeps the Chrism Mass entirely separate from the evening Last Supper Mass. It would be true to say that the whole of this Mass has been infected by the new theme of priesthood: the lections have been altered from James 5:13–16 (anointing the sick) and Mark 6:7–13 (the mission of the twelve) to Isaiah 61:1–3a,6a.8b-9 ("The Spirit of the Lord is upon me . . . "), Revelation 1:5–8 ("I am alpha and omega"), and Luke 4:16–21 (Jesus in the synagogue at Nazareth). While all these passages could refer to the

23. See Martimort, "La catéchèse de la bénédiction des saintes huiles," *La Maison-Dieu* 41 (1955) 69–72.

24. *The Sacramentary* 131–134. See P. Jounel, "La consécration du chrême et des saintes huiles," *La Maison-Dieu* 112 (1972) 70–83; but see also N. K. Rasmussen, "The Chrism Mass: Tradition and Renewal," in *The Cathedral: A Reader* (Washington,D.C.: United States Catholic Conference, 1979) 29–33.

whole people of God, the renewal of priestly vows after the homily marks off the ordained from the unordained, which many find appropriate, but others—Roman Catholic scholars included—do not. Those who like this new rite appreciate the opportunity of coming away from a busy parish at a busy time and reflecting together on the priesthood. Those who do not like this rite find it unnecessarily self-conscious, and may even see behind its introduction some of the internal disciplinary problems of the Roman Catholic Church's presbyterate in the late 1960s. It is interesting to note how the ordination theme dominates the collect and proper preface, which are entirely new compositions in order to bring the whole Mass into line with its new ingredient. The weakness of the collect is that it explicitly refers only to those ordained, thus marking off this prayer from practically every other collect in the new Missal, and certainly undermining the notion of the collect as being the first main prayer of the whole people of God as they gather for eucharistic worship.

The blessing of the oils can either occur in the traditional places, oil for the sick at the end of the eucharistic prayer and the other two oils after communion, though the oil of exorcism comes before the chrism; or else the blessings can be given after the liturgy of the word. Moreover, the chrism can be mixed at the service itself. Some commentators express the hope that this will be done, and will make chrism considerably more odorous than it has been in the past. The blessings have been largely rewritten so that they reflect more of what the oils are supposed to symbolize and do. The blessing of chrism has two alternatives, the old Gregorian prayer, and a new one which is strongly Christological and ecclesial in its tone.

Many Anglicans[25] warm to this new service, while oth-

25. A form for "Reaffirmation of Ordination Vows" (with Holy Thursday in view) appears in the Episcopalian *Book of Occasional Services* (New York: Seabury, 1979) 212–215. The text is clearly inspired by the 1970 *Missale Romanum*. See also Stevenson, "On Keeping Holy Week" 36ff.

ers suspect the renewal of priestly vows as being authoritarian in inspiration. The use of oil has long been an option in Anglican worship all over the world, and is on the increase. Similarly, there is a tendency for Anglicans to adapt the priestly vows into wider and more contemporary concepts of ministry within the church, and to permit such a reaffirmation on other occasions in the church's year. On the other hand, such "affirmations," baptismal as well as priestly, may be yet one more symptom of self-conscious Christianity today.

The Chrism Mass has, therefore, a somewhat ironical history. A rite originally belonging to the Easter Vigil eucharist, preparing and blessing the oils just before use, is transferred back to Holy Thursday in order to become part of the bishop's eucharist of the Last Supper. Then it becomes a separate eucharist in its own right, with elaborate blessings for the oils, now including the oil for anointing the sick. The blessings have been considerably simplified, but the eucharist has been given a new character altogether. Such is the western rite's *ingenium* for taking over a custom, expanding it, and fitting it into a new eucharist of its own.

Last Supper

The older Latin title was usually *Coena Domini* (the "supper of the Lord"), and the Roman liturgical books mark this eucharist as the beginning of the Triduum, thus implicitly downgrading the chrismal celebration as preparatory and not specifically to do with the celebration of the Paschal Triduum.[26] It has also been called *Natalis calicis* ("birthday of the eucharistic cup"). The survival of the English title is due in no small part to the Royal Maundy ceremony, itself a survival of the ancient practice of the sovereign washing the feet of ordinary people.[27] Those

26. See note 15.
27. See Tyrer, *Historical Survey of Holy Week* 111–112. It is still an annual event in the life of the British Sovereign.

44

who may criticize the custom of handing out special coins at Royal Maundy can perhaps take cold comfort in the inherent dangers of the liturgy becoming what used to be called "radical," "relevant," and "meaningful" (and usually very ephemeral).

The lections for this day are solidly consistent in the West, except that Cranmer adapted them unnecessarily for Anglicans. In the Roman and modern Anglican tradition the epistle is Paul's narrative of the supper (1 Cor 11:23–36) and the gospel is the foot washing (Jn 13:1–15). The new Roman rite adds an Old Testament lesson (Ex 12:1–8, 11–14), which was originally read on Good Friday and which has a strongly paschal typological flavor in its new context.[28]

It appears that the usual time for this Mass in the Middle Ages was 3:00 p.m., although this is late in the day in late spring in the Mediterranean world, when most work is done.[29] The growth of the evening eucharist in the last thirty years has had a great effect on Maundy Thursday, as previous practice in the Roman Catholic Church brought this celebration forward to the morning. For those of us used to evening eucharists week by week, it is hard to imagine how the average medieval peasant felt when walking to church in the late afternoon for Mass on this single occasion in the church's year.

Foot Washing

Three special customs soon become associated with this eucharist: the washing of feet, the procession of the sacrament, and the stripping of the altars. The three are obvious, but for different reasons. The washing of feet interprets the gospel. The procession of the sacrament removes the consecrated bread to a place where it can be kept for those who wish to receive communion at the end of the

---

28. *Ordo Lectionum Missae* 25.
29. Tyrer, *Historical Survey of Holy Week* 112–115.

Good Friday liturgy. And the stripping of the altar provides a unique opportunity for a thorough spring cleaning; it also symbolizes the deprivation of the church in having no eucharistic celebration until the Easter Vigil, and the desolation of the abandoned and crucified Lord. Here are three liturgical gems which require no explanation by anyone when they are carried out as liturgical ceremonies.

The foot washing originally took place after the eucharist, either before or after the stripping of the altars. The seventeenth Council of Toledo (694) waxes somewhat humorous in urging the custom to be observed:

> Partly through idleness, partly through custom, in certain churches the brethren's feet are not washed by priests during the services of Maundy Thursday, for which they plead no other excuse than traditional custom.[30]

Behind this admonition one can, perhaps, see an innovation which central authority is trying to press on others, or else, and more likely, an old custom which was dying out, probably because it hadn't become formalized within a liturgical framework. It appears to have been particularly popular after Mass in both East and West in religious communities, where perhaps it is both more natural and appropriate, particularly if the leading part is taken by the abbot. The Romano-Germanic Pontifical[31] provides a detailed and rich procedure, including a repeat of the Mass gospel and the entire Johannine farewell discourse (Jn 13:16–17:26), surely an endurance test which not even the most Protestant preacher would wish to inflict on a congregation. Later books avoid such excesses but give full provision for biblically inspired antiphons and responses to be sung during the ceremony. Foot washing is one of those symbols which is so near the bone that some people

30. Translation by Tyrer, *Historical Survey of Holy Week* 109; discussed by Beatrice, *La lavanda dei piedi* 205ff. and Schmidt, *Hebdomada Sancta* II 767ff.
31. See Schmidt, *Hebdomada Sancta* II 571–588.

feel uncomfortable unless it is stylized. Sometimes I wonder how religious communities feel while it is going on, particularly if there are acute tensions and disagreements among the brethren. Perhaps that is as well; it would be naive to talk glibly about self-acceptance without also realizing that amendment of life lies at the heart of the gospel.

One of the finest liturgical hymns of Holy Week finds its inspiration in the foot washing, the "Ubi Caritas," probably composed in a Benedictine monastery in Reichenau about 800.[32] It survives in the new Roman rite as a suggested hymn during the washing of feet. Since 1956 the foot washing is part of the eucharist itself and comes after the homily. The context may bluntly suggest to the preacher what form the discourse should take. The opening lines of the hymn run as follows:

> Where charity and love are found, there is God.
> The love of Christ has gathered us together into one.
> Let us rejoice and be glad in him.
> Let us fear and love the living God,
> and love each other from the depths of our heart.
> Where charity and love are found, there is God.

These themes are timeless in Christianity. Brian Wren has written a hymn along a similar theme, but which focuses more directly on the action of Christ.

> Lord God, in Christ you call our name,
>   and then receive us as your own,
> not through some merit, right, or claim,
>   but by your gracious love alone.
> We strain to glimpse your mercy-seat,
>   and find you kneeling at our feet.
>
> Then take the towel, and break the bread,
>   and humble us, and call us friends.
> Suffer and serve till all are fed,
>   and show us how grandly love intends

32. Text and discussion in Schmidt, *Hebdomada Sancta* II 651–653.

to work till all creation sings,
to fill all worlds, to crown all things.[33]

Here are words which resound, too, and suggest all kinds of nuances to the faithful who come "seeking hope for humankind," as the preceding stanza ends.

Communion for the Morrow?[34]

The eucharist for this day concludes on a note of emptiness and confidence, that uncanny blend of dysphoric and euphoric which the Holy Week liturgy somehow holds together. The sacrament was only taken somewhere else in the Roman rite from the seventh century onwards, as the practice of communicating on Good Friday, which began in the East, gained popularity. By the twelfth century only the priest usually received communion, but the great eucharistic compensation of that era, the cult of the sacrament, gave Maundy Thursday the impressive and tragic procession, in deep solemnity, of carrying the consecrated host to an altar of repose where the sacramental Christ should lie till the morrow. Aquinas' hymn for Corpus Christi, "Pange lingua gloriosi corporis," supplies the right mixture of strength in weakness with which to return from a decorated side-altar to a bare and stripped feasting-table:

> Word made Flesh, by word he maketh
> Very bread his Flesh to be;
> Man in wine Christ's blood partaketh:
> And if senses fail to see,
> Faith alone the true heart waketh
> To behold the mystery.[35]

33. Text in *Hymns Ancient and Modern New Standard* (1983) no. 489.
34. Discussion in Schmidt, *Hebdomada Sancta* II 798ff.
35. Text in *The New English Hymnal* (Norwich: The Canterbury Press, 1986) no. 268. Translation by J. M. Neale, E. Caswell, and others.

The eucharist is so often a case of bringing heaven and earth together. It was not for nothing that the compilers of the new Roman rite chose a beautiful old prayer as today's post-communion:

> Almighty God,
> we receive new life
> from the supper your Son gave us in this world.
> May we find full contentment
> in the meal we hope to share
> in your eternal kingdom.
> We ask this through Christ our Lord.[36]

The American Lutheran Book of Worship contains a liturgy for this day which combines two of the special themes of Holy Thursday—penitence and Last Supper. The eucharist begins with a sermon, which leads into a penitential rite of an extended nature. The liturgy of the word follows, and the optional foot washing may come after the gospel. The eucharistic liturgy is thus set within a peculiarly stark context on this occasion. A clever link is made between the sermon at the beginning and the act of penitence by a special address, which ends on a strongly eucharistic note:

> Remembering our Lord's last supper with his disciples,
> we eat the bread and share the cup of this meal.
> Together we receive the Lord's gift of himself and
> participate in that new covenant
>   which makes us one in him.
> The Eucharist is the promise of the great banquet
>   we will share
> with all the faithful, when our Lord returns,
>   the culmination
> of our reconciliation with God and each other.[37]

The Holy Land has an endless store of experiences for the Christian to enjoy and by which to be challenged. One

36. *The Sacramentary* 139. For sources, see A. Dumas, "Les sources du nouveau missel romain," *Notitiae* 61 (1971) 74.
37. *The Lutheran Book of Worship* (Minister's Desk Edition) 137ff.

of mine certainly comes to mind from that memorable holiday. My father and I undertook an ambitious journey which started in Jerusalem early in the morning and involved driving down to the Jordan, up the valley to Galilee, round the Sea of Tiberias, up into the hills around Nazareth, over to Haifa, down the coast of the Mediterranean to Caesarea, and thence back up the hill to Jerusalem. We celebrated his sixty-eighth birthday by having lunch near the waterfront at Tiberias itself. Everything was perfect. The sun was shining. There weren't too many tourists. And the menu was not even particularly expensive. We ordered a salad and Peter-fish, cooked on charcoal, and washed it down with Mount Carmel wine and pitta-bread. I reckon that I'm fairly hard-boiled about religious experiences. But at the time I noticed the two Jewish young men who served us, dark hair, with the little caps on their heads. They laughed and chatted with us and wanted us to enjoy ourselves. We didn't need much encouragement. But the meal which was served to us so readily and lovingly had a sacramental quality about it which is hard to describe; and so I won't go any further than that.

CHAPTER FOUR

OUTCAST OUTSIDE: CROSS AND REJECTION

Reproaches and the Cross

My people, what have I done to you?
How have I offended you? Answer me!

I led you out of Egypt, from slavery to freedom,
but you led your Saviour to the cross.

My people, what have I done to you?
How have I offended you? Answer me!

Holy is God! Holy and strong! Holy immortal one,
have mercy on us!

For forty years I led you safely through the desert.
I fed you with manna from heaven
and brought you to a land of plenty;
but you led your Saviour to the cross.

Holy is God! Holy and strong! Holy immortal one,
Have mercy on us!

What more could I have done for you?
I planted you as the fairest vine,
but you yielded bitterness:
when I was thirsty you gave me vinegar to drink
and you pierced your Saviour with a lance.

Holy is God! Holy and strong! Holy immortal one,
Have mercy on us.[1]

THE OLD WESTERN Good Friday liturgy is made up of a number of strange and exciting elements, at the heart of which is the veneration of the cross. During this ceremony hymns of devotion are usually sung, and the most traditional is this painful cry of reproach to the people of God. Never intended to be anti-Semitic, the Reproaches probably come from the ancient Spanish church, which used Micah 6:1–8 (the third verse makes up the opening reproach, "my people, what have I done to you?") on Good Friday; something resembling them appears to have been used on Good Friday at Jerusalem.[2] Great minds do think alike sometimes in composing new liturgies! There is something dynamically Christian about this chant. *Why* did you do it? Couldn't you *see* how futile it was? Sometimes it takes a persecuted people to see the full implications of this truth. Guido Rocha, a Brazilian artist, sculpted "The Tortured Christ" in 1975. It depicts the death-cry of Jesus in agony and expresses the strength of the Latin American church. Under the sculpture Rocha writes: "The characteristic of Christ is that his life was totally coherent, so coherent that the world could not stand him."[3] Those are perceptive words indeed, coming from someone who would not claim, in a formal sense, to be a Christian.

The cross has long fascinated people, and it even knows non-Christian uses. The slaughtered Passover lamb was

1. *The Sacramentary* 160–164.
2. Schmidt, *Hebdomada Sancta* II 791–796 (esp. 794). On the fifth-eighth century Jerusalem rite, see M. Tarchnischvili, *Le Grand lectionnaire de l'Eglise de Jerusalem (Vè-VIIIè siècle)* II, C.S.C.O. 205, Scriptores Iberici 14 (Louvain: Secrétariat du Corpus Scriptorum Christianorum Orientalium, 1960) 105ff. (no. 703) and 108ff. (no. 114). [See attempt at non-"anti-Semitic" text in (Church of England) *Lent Holy Week and Easter: Services and Prayers* (London: Church House Publishing/Cambridge University Press/S.P.C.K., 1986) 207ff.].
3. Hans Ruedi-Weber, *On a Friday Noon—Meditations on the Cross* (London: S.P.C.K., 1979) 79.

placed on two platters, in the form of a cross. The cross was a means of ignominious execution. These two backgrounds provide Christianity with the means whereby the symbol has been monopolized, but not in a triumphalistic sense. Rather, we are a group of people who are almost haunted by that symbol because it has a power and a meaning which we are supposed to try to appropriate and make our own. There can be no Christian faith without the cross. It is interesting that the actor Robert Powell, who took the part of Jesus in the Zeffirelli film "Jesus of Nazareth," finds Jesus' teaching in the Sermon on the Mount the most powerful aspect of his life. But it is impossible to avoid the effect on any actor of the crucifixion itself. While it has its unhealthy possibilities (who can "act Christ"?), it nonetheless brings with it so much baggage, in the way of people's expectations as they watch the play or film, that the actor must come to terms somehow with a scene which has not exhausted two thousand years' worth of poetry, drama, art, music—and liturgy.

History, however, continues to surprise us, for the early Christians found no use in depicting the cross. It is not until the fourth century and after that Christians went in for depicting the cross in a big way. Tradition has it that Elena, Emperor Constantine's mother, "found" the cross at Golgotha in 335.[4] And, as we shall see later, the ceremonial veneration of the cross originates in the Jerusalem liturgy. Why the change? Many reasons can be offered. But just as we must beware of distinguishing too glibly between pre-fourth century and post-fourth century worship, so we must avoid assuming that the cross did not feature at all before it was allegedly found by that holy woman in 335.

The fact is that Christian writers and teachers grappled with the cross right through those early centuries. Moreover, it is likely that "veneration of the cross" in Jerusalem owed more to a strong tradition of Christians praying to

4. Wilkinson, *Egeria's Travels* 240ff.

53

Christ as the crucified one who will return in glory from the East. Popular piety so often brings together realities which later theology separates. Early Syriac piety suggests that this crucified and worshiped Lord who would return to the church at the end is the real precursor of the veneration of the cross.[5] The East again! The Spanish and French liturgists who put together the Reproaches had already borrowed the eastern *Trisagion* hymn, "Holy is God, Holy and strong, Holy immortal one, have mercy on us" which comes near the start of the Byzantine Mass. To place it as the popular response to these Good Friday Reproaches sets the right penitential tone for the day. We are not here to tear ourselves apart, nor yet to pity Jesus. We are here to contemplate the greatness of God's love in the most paradoxical action that any religion knows. On Palm Sunday we read as the epistle an early Christian hymn (Phil 2:5–11) which sums it all up; he humbled himself, in spite of all, and God has exalted him, so that his ordinary name becomes a proper one, which human history can neither forget nor eradicate. The crucifixion is too deeply embedded in the corporate memory of Christians. There is so much else that we can fruitfully forget, or else deliberately relegate to the margins. The cross of Christ lies at the heart of creation.

This means that our celebration of Good Friday can never degenerate into being a religious routine. Whatever our particular emphasis, it is central to the faith. Whether it is the agonized Christ of that Brazilian sculptor; the stylized Christ who hangs in shame against a divine golden background in eastern iconography; the Romanesque Christ who stands, fully clad, combining suffering and glory; the later medieval tendency to bring contemporary characters and problems into the whole passion drama— the options continue to be open, and the odds are that both within and outside the community of faith, that sym-

5. See Bernard Capelle, "Aux origines du culte de la croix," *Travaux Liturgiques* III (Louvain: Centre Liturgique, 1967) 215–220.

bol with its saving criminal on it will fascinate the creative forces of human beings for a long time to come.[6] The hymn writer, too, can capture a dimension to the story which the preacher and the painter cannot. Thus Venantius Fortunatus (*Vexilla regis prodeunt*—"The royal banners forward go") uses the imagery of royalty and glory to show just how incredible is the mercy of God shown to us by Jesus' life and death. How right for the sixth century West, the Roman Empire having crumbled! Much later, Paul Gerhardt's "O Haupt voll Blut und Wenden" ("O sacred head, surrounded by crown of piercing thorn") can reveal the reality and the hope of the cross in the middle of the seventeenth century, in the bloodshed of the Thirty Years' War. In our own country the evangelical Isaac Watts still holds the stage with his staggering "When I survey the wondrous cross," which few of its customary singers realize was originally intended to be used at the eucharist.[7]

The Cross and Spirituality

But all that art still has its limitations. It relies a bit too much on the ability and insight of the artist, and on the openness and judgment of the rest of the community. The Christian faith, above all the Christian cross, is something to be *celebrated*, and much as we can hover fruitfully before the cross, it still comes down to the need to *worship*, and to worship *together*. I remember being severely critical of Good Friday services when I was a boy. Too often the mood was drab and dreary—and often *mood* can poison reality in a service in a way that *text* cannot correct. To give in and produce tired and lifeless worship on this day of all days is a little like avoiding a challenge which God himself is giving us. While liturgy continues to evolve and

6. See Ruedi-Weber, *On a Friday Noon*, passim.
7. See M. Frost, ed., *Historical Companion to Hymns Ancient and Modern* (London: Clowes, 1962) 187, 198ff., 196ff.

change, there must be certain constants. Jesus died, a fact which even non-Christian historians agree; but he died in a particular context, as a Jew who was accused of blasphemy after a ministry of doing God's work, covertly as well as openly. The context is provided by the gospels themselves, which devote more space to the passion than they do to anything else. They do this in different ways, and what more evidence have we that Christians have realized this for centuries than in the simple fact that they used to take such care in reading all four passion narratives in Holy Week? Within the New Testament we can already see signs of deep reflection on the meaning of Christ's death.[8] That is why preaching the cross has occupied such a central position in Christianity, whether in Jesuit-inspired devotions as the "Three Hours," with sermons on those "seven words from the cross," or in using that slot after the Johannine passion narrative as an opportunity for presenting the old, old story in a way that helps to bring the congregation to its knees.

Suffering is easy to discuss but more difficult to redeem; and in our century, which lives under the threat of nuclear catastrophe, with millions unemployed, and a frustrated utilitarianism at the back of many of our communities, it is too easy to be bland about God "sending suffering," and doling out the cross as if it's a divine blank check to cover the cost of all the pain and inconvenience and nausea which we have to face. There is a lot of suffering which *need* not happen. There is a lot of suffering which *must* happen.[9] Perhaps if Christians were prepared to suffer more, then other kinds of suffering which are unnecessary could be dealt with and avoided. Yet all this should not lead us into an orgy of self-pity. It should rather help us to come before God, having purged ourselves of non-

8. See Chapter One, note 3.
9. For a discussion of this issue, see Rowan Williams, *Resurrection: Interpreting the Easter Gospel* (London: Darton, Longmann, and Todd, 1982) esp. 52ff.

essentials so that we are ready to become a living sacrifice. Good Friday is a day of *celebration* and *intercession*.

Egeria and After

Our own story must take up Egeria's narrative once more. You may remember that we left her and her motley array of pilgrims at Gethsemane in the early hours of Friday morning. The long processional services continue with a walk into the city to the main church, at the point where the crucifixion was supposed to have taken place, Golgotha; here the account of the trial of Jesus before Pilate is read (Jn 18:28–19:16). The bishop then encourages the people to stay the course: "they have been hard at it all night, and there is further effort in store for them in the day ahead," writes Egeria, with her personal and sympathetic touch. But they are actually sent home for some rest and told to return at about eight o'clock, when they will be able to see "the holy Wood of the Cross," as it is formally called. She takes up the narrative as follows:

> It is not long before everyone is assembled for the next service. The bishop's chair is placed on Golgotha Behind the Cross (the cross there now), and he takes his seat. A table is placed before him with a cloth on it, the deacons stand round, and there is brought to him a gold and silver box containing the holy Wood of the Cross. It is opened, and the Wood of the Cross and the Title are taken out and placed on the table.
>
> As long as the holy Wood is on the table, the bishop sits with his hands resting on either end of it and holds it down, and the deacons round him keep watch over it. They guard it like this because what happens now is that all the people, catechumens as well as faithful, come up one by one to the table. They stoop down over it, kiss the Wood, and move on. But on one occasion (I don't know when) one of them bit off a piece of the holy Wood and stole it away, and for this reason the deacons stand round

and keep watch in case anyone dares to do the same again. Thus all the people go past one by one. They stoop down, touch the holy Wood first with their forehead and then with their eyes, and then kiss it, but no one puts out his hand to touch it.[10]

This local ceremony goes on until midday, which means that it lasts a few hours. It is not a formal liturgy, for there are no hymns or chants or readings. But the act of veneration is placed within a context, because the people have been going to services at various points, and they will be going to more. But Egeria's account gives us no suggestion of stylization. Care is taken to protect the cross-relic from being stolen or from being damaged by the over-zealous. Egeria takes care to tell us all, because this is one of those ceremonies with which she is totally unfamiliar.

When this is over, the faithful gather Before the Cross, a tight space in the main building, where from noon until three o'clock in the afternoon, there takes place a service which is made up mainly of readings, both of psalms, epistles, and gospels, all concerned with the sufferings of Christ. Egeria hints that the Old Testament lections included prophecies of his suffering (Is 52 and 53—the suffering servant—spring to mind as an obvious candidate) as well as the passion narratives. Her description of this word service is interesting:

> For those three hours, then, they are teaching the people that nothing which took place had not been foretold, and all that was foretold was completely fulfilled; and between all the readings are prayers, all of them appropriate to the day.

Egeria is clearly struck by the emotions of the congregation during this liturgy, and she notes that

> when three o'clock comes, they have the reading from St. John's Gospel about Jesus giving up the ghost, and, when that has been read, there is a prayer, and the dismissal.

10. Wilkinson, *Egeria's Travels* 136ff.

The day ends with a service at the Anastasis (the tomb): the main feature is the narrative of the burial of Christ (Mt 27:57–61). There is no vigil-litany, because the people are too tired, and they have the morrow to face as well.[11]

Conservatism operates once again. The Armenian lectionary which dates from the fifth century in Jerusalem fills out Egeria's narrative, particularly at the three hours' office, and it also directs that the "wood of the cross" should be placed on Golgotha for veneration all through the morning. But the scheme has become simplified in one way and elaborated in another by the time of the Georgian lectionary a few centuries later, which still has the veneration of the cross. However, the liturgy begins at noon and is made up of twelve readings and chants, whereas the fifth century rite had no fewer than twenty.[12] After these come the evening hymn of light, the *phos hilaron*, the Lord's Prayer, the "burial of the cross," and the liturgy of the presanctified.

It is a more formal rite than its predecessors, and one which is perhaps more "popular" in its appeal: readings and chants, Lord's Prayer, cross-ceremony, and presanctified liturgy. For venerating the relic substitute burial of "the" cross and insert communion from the reserved sacrament. The origins of this method of receiving communion are not clear. It was probably a result of hermits and holy people taking the sacrament home with them for their use during the week between one eucharist and another. We know that at the end of the seventh century the Byzantine rite declared all days of Lent, except Saturday, Sundays, and the Annunciation, to be "aliturgic," namely, days on which the eucharist was not to be celebrated, but when the presanctified liturgy could be administered. The East has always placed great store on the centrality of the eucharist, but it has done so in ways different from the

11. See note 10 above.

12. Wilkinson, *Egeria's Travels* 267. For the Georgian lectionary, see note 2 above.

West. This Jerusalem Good Friday custom would have been familiar to the pilgrim, certainly the eastern pilgrims. It would not have been something special: Good Friday gets a presanctified liturgy in the same way that most weekdays of Lent might, thus adding to the penitential character of Good Friday.

In the West similar conservatism and austerity operate. There is no eucharist. Innocent I forbids it in his letter to Decentius in 416.[13] The Sixteenth Council of Toledo (693) likewise forbids it.[14] But what we have in the old Roman rite is a different kind of museum piece, which has altered very little through the centuries. Without any opening collect, there is an Old Testament reading (Hos 6:1–6); all that introduces it is the entry of the ministers who prostrate themselves before the altar. After a chant, another Old Testament lection follows (Ex 12:1–11, now read on Maundy Thursday), which in turn leads into a chant and then the climax of the liturgy of the word, that is, the reading of the passion according to St. John (Jn 18). These lead into the solemn prayers, which are a series of intercessions consisting of biddings and collects, each one on a particular theme.

The Solemn Prayers

The German liturgist, Anton Baumstark, wrote an important book called *Comparative Liturgy* in which he attempted to work out the method which the liturgist could bring to the trade when looking at liturgies from a comparative standpoint.[15] One of the "laws" he promulgated was that liturgy is more resistant to change on special occasions. We have had several examples so far. This Good Friday rite is also a clear example: some readings, interspersed with chants, and then the intercessions. In

13. See Cabié, *La lettre du pape Innocent Ier* 24ff.
14. See Tyrer, *Historical Survey* 119.
15. See A. Baumstark, *Liturgie Comparée* (Chevetogne, 1953) 30.

most of the modern western liturgies today the intercession has been "restored" to its original position, between the word and the start of the eucharist itself. An analysis of these old Roman intercessions reveals that the biddings probably date from the third century and that the collects are from the later fourth century.[16] Further conclusions are offered that the intercessions do not belong solely to the Good Friday liturgy, but were once part of the Roman Mass itself, but were dislodged due to a number of other factors, such as the growth of the pre-Mass litany, the intercession within the canon or eucharistic prayer, and the increasing number of Masses celebrated normally. The first bidding and collect have changed little over the centuries. Here are the texts in the 1970 Missal:

> Let us pray, dear friends,
> for the holy Church of God throughout the world,
> that God the almighty father
> guide it and gather it together
> so that we may worship him
> in peace and tranquility.

> Almighty and eternal God,
> you have shown your glory to all nations
> in Christ, your Son.
> Guide the work of your Church.
> Help it to persevere in faith,
> proclaim your name,
> and bring your salvation to people everywhere.[17]

One of the noticeable features of modern liturgy is that the intercessions are frequently led by people who compose their own prayers, whether from recognized sources or in their own words. The Roman Missal itself provides

---

16. See G. G. Willis, *Essays in Early Roman Liturgy*, Alcuin Club Collections 46, (London: S.P.C.K., 1964) 1–48; and P. De Clerck, *La "Prière Universelle" dans les Liturgies Latines Anciennes: Témoignages Patristiques et Textes Liturgiques*, Liturgiewissenschaftliche Quellen und Forschungen 62 (Münster: Aschendorff, 1977).

17. *The Sacramentary* 151.

surprisingly little help, although Anglican books suggest patterns and forms, usually in the sequence of church, world, community, suffering, departed, saints. Many churches enjoy this development and do it well. There may be a group of people who are gifted in this respect: they can submit themselves to the discipline of stringing words together in such a way as to suggest lines of thought and prayers to the congregation. But there are pitfalls. I remember once attending a eucharist in the course of whose intercessions the number of items and intentions and biddings which concerned the church (the first section) far outnumbered the corresponding items and intentions and biddings for all the rest put together. What kind of impression would that convey to the chance visitor with ears open? A community intent upon itself, and perhaps lacking social concern, awareness of the ministry of healing, and many other interests in addition to these?

The genius of this ancient combination of bidding and collect is that, at least originally, the bidding can be *free* and *specific* (and, let's admit it, *short*), whereas the collect can be set and general in its scope. Moreover, where two or more voices are used, these solemn intercessions can be an effective device for learning the spirituality of intercession. The biddings, led by one person, suggest specific topics, and only a few. Silence follows, for the congregation to assimilate these and to think its own deep thoughts. Then the theme in question is summarized in a prayer of general character which offers this part of the whole intercession to God's care and protection. The difference between the bidding and the collect is that the bidding is addressed to the congregation whereas the collect is addressed to God. Now, I am not a believer of things ancient for the sake of being ancient, although I think it is good for the church's liturgy to contain some elements which go back to early times. But this old form of intercession has a great deal to teach the western churches today at a time when intercessory prayer is in danger of being trivialized beyond recognition. How often do intercessions induce the reaction of "Let us pray—here is the news"? How often are intercessions yet one more example of the church indulging in navel-gazing? How often are intercessions the kernel of well-intentioned actions but bad theology? How often do we slip into our own little clichés, which may irritate others intensely? I am making a plea for these solemn prayers to be used on other occasions, or at any rate for something resembling them to be used frequently in the church's year. They spell out the meaning of intercession, and they convey its essentially *sacrificial* character.[18] Intercession is no mere verbalization. It is part of the priestly work of the whole church, and we offer ourselves as a living sacrifice to God. That is why these old prayers, or something like them, follow on so tellingly from the reading of the passion according to St. John.

The topics can vary. One of the first actions of Pope John XXIII was to alter the old prayer for Christian unity, which was obviously aimed at patristic heretics, and which spoke in bombastic terms of those outside what some people still call "Catholic unity." The 1970 sequence is slightly different from the 1570 Missal and the 1956 Order produced under Pius XII. After the prayer for the unity of the church, prayers are offered for Jews (no longer anti-Semitic in overtones), for those who do not know Christ, for unbelievers, and then for leaders of state, and for those in trouble. It is remarkable that the spirit of the Second Vatican Council should leave its mark on this old sequence of prayers, and thereby provide the church with a new kind of self-understanding, as the community offers intercession on this solemn day.[19]

In many modern rites the intercessions can vary, of course, but the lections remain constant. There is a ten-

18. See Kenneth Stevenson, " 'Ye Shall Pray For': The Intercession," in Stevenson, ed., *Liturgy Reshaped* (London: S.P.C.K., 1982) 32–47.
19. *The Sacramentary* 151–155. Widely found in other modern service books, often with some discreet variations.

dency to have Isaiah 52:13–53:12 (the suffering servant) as the Old Testament lesson; and to read Hebrews 4:14–16 and 5:7–9 (Christ as high priest, passed into the heavens) as the second reading, which used to be read in the Good Friday offices. For the Johannine passion narrative, the same dramatic possibilities obtained, and obtain today, for different voices and various kinds of musical participation.[20]

Veneration of the Cross

The intercessions ended, we now come to the veneration of the cross. How it travelled west from Jerusalem is not hard to guess; the pilgrims probably brought it. At the end of the eighth century, a Roman "ordo" (description of services) gives us a very eastern-looking Good Friday service. The bishop leads the procession, carrying a thurible, with which he incenses the cross. The liturgy begins with the veneration of the cross, after which the word service follows. A later ordo has the veneration after the synaxis or word service, when the cross is placed on the altar and venerated. During the latter, the antiphon *Ecce lignum crucis* ("Behold, the wood of the cross") and Psalm 118 (119) are sung.[21]

What has happened here is that the "wood of the cross" has ceased to be a relic but is a sort of liturgical code-word for any cross used by a local church on this occasion. Many Christians did purport to have a real regular relic; and one can imagine that the number of these relics would probably make up enough wood to fill many a Scandinavian forest. But the verities of these claims are not strictly relevant. The veneration of the cross has arrived in Rome; it is also found in the Spanish and French traditions.

20. See Schmidt, *Hebdomada Sancta* II 679–683 for history. Modern service books make elaborate revisions, e.g., *Lent Holy Week Easter: Services and Prayers* 142–175.
21. See *Ordines Romani* 16, 17, 23, 24, 31 (texts in Schmidt, *Hebdomada Sancta* II 507.

But the way it arrives at Rome betrays the oriental origins. No self-respecting Roman bishop ever walks in procession, and at the *head* of a procession, with a thurible. Moreover, there is more "logic" in venerating the cross *after* the synaxis, thus making it the quasi-sacramental action of the day. By "logic" I mean that western tendency to adopt new customs but make them tidy, for there is nothing particularly liturgical and tidy in Egeria's account of the veneration. It is ironical that a ceremony which starts life in Jerusalem should spread west but then drop out of the eastern program altogether. Whether other parts of the West got the veneration from Rome, or whether Spain and France gave it to Rome, is not clear. What is clear is that this local Jerusalem rite fascinated enough minds to fill the liturgical trade-route. Psalm 118 (119) is a lengthy meditation on the "law" of spiritual growth, penitence and renewal, which is easily christianized, particularly when the faithful are confronted with the "law" of the cross. But those Reproaches soon worm their way into the western rites. The main part appears in a later ninth century antiphonal from Senlis in France. The second part, which begins "for your sake I scourged your captors," was added in the later Middle Ages, so extending the theme of reproach and salvation.[22]

Today modern rites allow various options. "Creeping to the Cross,"[23] as it was called in the English Middle Ages, is a custom which Protestants on the whole fear less than they used to, although where veneration is done, it is frequently a slightly truncated rite whereby the faithful kneel down where they are during the singing of hymns and the recitation of prayers addressed to a large cross at the far end of the church. But however that veneration is performed (and it is bound to be a matter of culture and spirituality), the real veneration goes on in the heart of the believer. The American Lutheran liturgy for this day has

22. See note 2 above.
23. Tyrer, *Historical Survey of Holy Week* 131.

a simple form of veneration. A "rough-hewn cross" is either in place before the liturgy starts or it is carried in procession into church after the solemn prayers. The veneration consists of silent meditations and appropriate hymnody.

Communion Today?

Finally, the Good Friday liturgy includes in many places the liturgy of the presanctified.[24] In the West, it is a peculiarity of the Roman tradition. It does not appear in the old Spanish and French books, nor even in the Milanese liturgies. It begins its life, it seems, in the seventh and eighth centuries, which prescribe that the consecrated bread be brought from the sacristy to the altar. The celebrant then takes up the Mass from the Lord's Prayer onwards, and distributes to the communicants. Two early books provide for communion in both kinds, reserved from the night before in this manner. Some of them later on restrict communion in both kinds to the celebrant. Later service books still reserve in one kind but provide a chalice with wine, which is supposed to be consecrated by dropping a particle of the consecrated host into it after the Lord's Prayer during the commixture. Early texts suggest that communion was only given to those who wanted it, and that it was not universally popular. Decline in regular communion resulted in elaborate processions to and from the place of repose, answering the increasing complexity of the deposition of the sacrament on the day before. The thirteenth century provides a full form for this procession in the Pontifical of Durandus of Mende. It is not until recently that popular communion on Good Friday has happened, probably for the first time ever.

24. On history, see sources cited above in note 21; see also Schmidt, *Hebdomada Sancta* II 797ff. E. Fischer suggested that the Mass of the presanctified might be abandoned, since there might be little enthusiasm on the part of the faithful to receive communion on this day, *La Maison-Dieu* 37 (1954) 118.

But there are two alternatives which history gives us. The first is to be found in the eighth century Gelasian sacramentaries, which combine the veneration of the cross with this communion, so that the faithful walk up towards the altar, venerate the cross, and receive communion at once.[25] This has the practical advantage of avoiding two lengthy queues. It has the theological advantage of giving a close connection between veneration and communion, which is the only time nowadays when the faithful will communicate in church in this way—unlike the East where the presanctified liturgy in the Byzantine rite is a regular practice, throughout Lent, after vespers. It is, perhaps, a pity that the Gelasian Sacramentary, which was followed in the practice of multiplying the Thursday Masses, was not also followed in bringing veneration and communion into one sacramental action.

The second alternative stems from the Reformation, where in Anglican and Lutheran traditions Good Friday has been observed as a day on which the eucharist was celebrated in its entirety. In a way, this departs radically from tradtion, but why is the tradition there? It could be said that if you have a eucharist on Thursday and the Saturday, you might as well have one on Friday. On this reckoning, the presanctified liturgy is a quaint survival, a means whereby Christians can have their cake and eat it too. The weakness of this particular Protestant observance lies not so much in its departure from tradition as in its tendency to reduce the eucharist to the cross only, thus denying it of its fully paschal tone. The question remains an open one, especially as modern rites from Anglican sources tend to allow all three options: no communion at

25. Tyrer, *Historical Survey of Holy Week* 29. See also A. Chavasse, *Le Sacramentaire Gélasien (Vaticanus Reginensis 316)*, Bibliothèque de Théologie Série IV, Histoire de la Théologie I (Paris: Desclée, 1957) 88–95. But there seems no confusion whatever in the Gelasian synthesis at this point, unless it be approached with a Gregorian "arrière-pensée."

all; a full eucharist; and the liturgy of the presanctified. The American Lutheran Book of Worship has no communion at all, as it makes the veneration of the cross the liturgical climax.

Other Options

In the East, the presanctified liturgy and the veneration of the cross, although adopted in the West, drop out of the Byzantine rite.[26] The burial of the cross, which was mentioned in the later Jerusalem rite, gives rise to an extension of the Good Friday liturgy so that the Christian contemplates not only the crucifixion but also the burial of Christ. In both the Syrian and Byzantine rites, there are attendant ceremonies which ritualize this crucial aspect of human experience. In the Byzantine tradition, a silk sheet depicting the burial of Christ is brought from the sanctuary at the end of vespers, together with the gospel book. Eventually it is brought to the place of "burial," a decorated tomb, where the faithful venerate it. The West imitated this practice, not with the *epitaphion*, but with a crucifix, and this is why many medieval churches contain "Easter sepulchers." Sometimes, as at Sarum, the burial included a consecrated host, and the tomb was locked. Such visual celebrations are not unrelated to death itself. Ambrose Verheul, the Abbot of Mont César at Louvain in Belgium, has recently suggested that a similar custom should be revived, in order to give point to the fact of Jesus' burial.[27] He thinks that it would make a suitable liturgy of the word on the morning of Easter Eve, and he notes how the themes of the burial, the resting of Christ, and the descent to the dead are so central to the Christian

26. For a discussion of the Byzantine rite on this day, see I.-H. Dalmais, "Le *Triduum Sacrum* dans la liturgie byzantine," *La Maison-Dieu* 41 (1955), 118ff.

27. See A. Verheul, "Le Mystère du Samedi Saint," *Questions Liturgiques* 65 (1984) 19–38. On the history of this rite, see Hardison, *Christian Rite and Christian Drama* 134ff.

tradition, and are a part of spiritual experience. Whatever one may think of this inspired analysis, Verheul has undoubtedly drawn attention to an important gap in the liturgical program by suggesting such a "representational" liturgy for this occasion.

All this traditional liturgy, whether fossilized or revamped, does not give the whole picture. The fact is that for many people devotions like the "Stations of the Cross,"[28] another Jerusalem inspired rite invented by the Franciscans, give the "events" of Holy Week an immediate and human character which the more intellectual, highbrow, and monastic liturgy embodies in the readings, intercessions, veneration of the cross, and the communion of the celebrant. The "Three Hours Devotion," so popular in the later nineteenth century and down to recent years, was invented at the end of the seventeenth century in no less a place than Lima in Peru.[29]

Good Friday is a composite picture made up of events, reflections, reactions, responses, all kinds of human ways of bringing the divine acts of God in Christ into our experience. Part of it is simply a matter of following through the gospels the path which Christ took. Part of it is halting at certain stages in that path and pondering the depths of the love which is shown to us then and now. Part of it is a re-enactment of a drama which is beyond human telling, and yet which inspires devotion in the faithful, the seeker, the half-believer, the outsider. We may well continue to ask what was going through Jesus' mind as he hung there, looking down over the city which rejected him, the city which loved him from afar, the city which was more than a symbol of God's presence with his people. The Roman rite ends with a prayer which sums up all that we can say:

Almighty and eternal God,
you have restored us to life

28. H. Thurston, *The Stations of the Cross: An Account of Their History and Devotional Purpose* (London: Longmans, 1906).
29. Tyrer, *Historical Survey of Holy Week* 141ff.

by the triumphant death and resurrection of Christ.
Continue this healing work within us.
May we who participate in this mystery
never cease to serve you.[30]

But where is the cross? In Jerusalem there are some
options. At this place or that in the church of the Sepulcher; or at the Garden Tomb, jealously guarded by Anglicans outside the new city. I remember a monk leading us
down into a new area of excavation, proudly showing us
the work that was going ahead, probing further and further underneath the crud left behind by those crusaders.
But while it was obviously an impressive exercise, it did
not answer the fundamental question, nor could it. As
we went down in the dark, we weren't looking for the
cross. The cross was everywhere, because you cannot lo-
cate it, neither in Jerusalem, nor in the liturgy, nor even
in the heart of the most devoted follower of the Man of
Sorrows. The cross, it seems, is too big to be contained
anywhere. It is eternal, in the mind of God from the beginning, the same God whom Jesus comes to show us, a God
who goes on loving and healing, even in the face of rejection.

30. *The Sacramentary* 167. For sources, see Chapter Two, note 36.

CHAPTER FIVE

OUTCAST REBORN: WATCH AND RENEWAL

The Queen of Seasons

Come, ye faithful, raise the strain
  Of triumphant gladness;
God hath brought his Israel
  Into joy from sadness;
Loosed from Pharaoh's bitter yoke
  Jacob's sons and daughters;
Led them with unmoistened foot
  Through the Red Sea waters.

'Tis the Spring of souls to-day;
  Christ hath burst his prison,
And from the three days' sleep in death
  As a Sun hath risen;
All the winter of our sins,
  Long and dark, is flying
From his Light, to whom we give
  Laud and praise undying.

Now the Queen of seasons, bright
  With the Day of splendour,
With the royal Feast of feasts,
  Comes its joy to render;
Comes to glad Jerusalem,
  Who with true affection
Welcomes in unwearied strains
  Jesu's Resurrection.

Neither might the gates of death,
Nor the tomb's dark portal,
Nor the watchers, nor the seal,
Hold thee as a mortal;
But to-day amidst the twelve
Thou didst stand, bestowing
That thy peace which evermore
Passeth human knowing.[1]

SO WROTE JOHN OF DAMASCUS in the eighth century, with the collapse of Byzantine Christianity imminent around him. It is quite an affirmation of the reality of God as one who raised Jesus and raises us. So strong and powerful is it that I sometimes regret that we have so much choice in our hymnody in the West today. Many other fine Easter hymns come to mind. Michael Weise's "Christus ist erstanden"; the old Latin "Ad regias Agni dapes," perhaps in the translation "At the Lamb's high feast we sing"; and Nikolai Grundtvig, the nineteenth century Danish hymn writer, presses all the natural imagery which is a feature of hymnody in that country to the very limits in a hymn addressed to the passion-flower, "Paskeblomst, hvad vil du her?" ("Passion-flower, what will you here?").[2]

But John of Damascus combines many of these ideas and it is a happy coincidence that he comes down to us in a translation made by John Mason Neale, to whom we owe a great deal in popularizing so many of the classical hymns of the East and West. It comes across particularly well when sung to the sixteenth century German melody from Leisentritts's "Gesangbuch." The hymn opens with a call to God's people to rejoice because they have been delivered from Pharaoh; Easter and Passover stand in rela-

1. See Frost, *Historical Companion to Hymns Ancient and Modern* 213ff.
2. *Den Danske Salmebog,* no. 206. See also Christian Thodberg, "Grundtvig the Hymnwriter," in Christian Thodberg, Anders Pontoppidan Thyssen, *N.F.S. Grundtvig: Tradition and Renewal* (Copenhagen: The Danish Institute, 1983) 160–196.

tion to each other, and the Red Sea rings bells with baptism as the fount from which we are cleansed and reborn. The Israelites were not drowned in it, but we are, and we live on. Then we sing of Jesus' "sleep in death," contrasting his burial with the long dark winter and the arrival of spring. One can also imagine the relief of the resurrection after the rigors of Holy Week worship! After that theme, Christians are invited to reflect on this "Queen of seasons," the "Feast of feasts," no doubt a eucharistic allusion; and Jerusalem is the place from which this celebration shines out "from his Light" (in the previous verse). Finally, the hymn provides a picture, or rather, two pictures: one is of Jesus standing above the tomb, with the guards and the seal unable to withstand the power of God; the other is of Jesus with the twelve, giving them the peace of God which passes all understanding. The four verses cover a great deal of ground.

The last verse brings to mind a fourteenth century reredos in Bohemia by an unknown local artist simply called "The Master of Trebon."[3] Its theme is the passion, and the central panel depicts the resurrection in a way that holds together the reality of the cross and the fullness of the resurrection. That central truth, in art, worship, piety, or theology, must prevent our celebration of Easter from degenerating into a "happy ending." So Jesus stands on but slightly over the tomb, with a faint suggestion of him slipping off. He wears a red cloak, matching the bloody skyline behind him. He holds a simple, tall, thin cross, which asserts itself on the tomb. He holds up his right hand in blessing. Round the tomb crouch four people who are obviously guards, looking in amazement and not bothering to hold their weapons, which, by the way, are up-to-date for the time. A craggy landscape ends in the distance with trees; nature is not allowed to let the Easter experience become no more than a psychological uplift.

3. See Anthony Rhodes, *Art Treasures of Eastern Europe* (London: Weidenfeld and Nicolson, 1972) 91.

It is useless trying to describe a painting, otherwise there would be no point in painting it. An effective painting of a religious kind has a number of points to make, some of which are clear, others of which are only suggested, and then there are many other ideas which just fade away. Liturgy is like that, too. There are central points of reference, and there are secondary features, and then there are background subtleties. The important aspect of all this should be that the central features remain central, and that the others are allowed their place but do not vie with the central character. Yet the whole business has got to be allowed its own life and liberty to grow and develop; and two of the criticisms commonly hurled at modern liturgies are that they are ephemeral and follow trendy ways, and that they are so ancient that they have nothing to say to our century. We are all finding it hard to use modern liturgies because of the debates that have gone on and continue to go on about what should be in them.[4] In the Church of England, you have the prospect of a bureaucracy with open politics writing our services. In the Roman Catholic Church the politics have been much less open, but they have been there nonetheless; a study-group made up of different kinds of liturgists, theologians, dignitaries, and Curial officials; drafts submitted and discussed between representatives of the study-group and more Curial officers. All this often results in the same kinds of compromise that other churches know. Unsatisfactory as many of the official rites are, whatever their origin, I think we have to learn to use them more imaginatively and pray them more effectively, not least of all in Holy Week, in our celebration of the "spring of souls." One of the ways we can do this is to appreciate, even relearn, the use of symbolism in worship, and Holy Week

4. See, for example, Bryan Spinks, "Liturgical Stock-Taking," *Theology* 90 (1987) 33–38.

is saturated with symbols, even if they are only "verbal" symbols, in the kind of Reformation piety which places its emphasis on readings and hymnody, or the Counter-Reformation piety which relies heavily on the Stations of the Cross and the Three Hours Devotion. The reason why we find symbolism awkward is not just because historians (like me) have exposed the varied and sometimes contradictory nature of the early and later evidence. The main reason is that because of the cult of liturgy as an exercise in education or therapy, we are in danger of neutering the whole exercise.[5]

Those who want the liturgy to be educational want to predetermine what the liturgy means and what it will teach the faithful. Thus we can come out of church asking each other "what have I learned this morning?" Educationally-minded presidents want to explain everything. I have witnessed the most excruciating liturgies when a well-intentioned priest has gabbled at such length about the "meaning" of "what we are about to do" that the symbolic act lay on the floor rather liked a pulped garlic. On the other side, those who want liturgy to be therapeutic will have a strongly anthropocentric view of the liturgical action, so that whatever else it does, it must do you good, build you up, heal you, enable you to get rid of your hang-ups. Therapy-minded presidents will be conscious of the dynamics of the group, where everyone is seated, and may even be quite dictatorial, in a manipulative fashion, about what is to go on in the service.

5. See in general Aidan Kavanagh, *Elements of Rite: A Handbook of Liturgical Style* (New York: Pueblo, 1982). The standard of public worship in our churches would be immeasurably improved were this remarkable little book to be made compulsory reading for all who go anywhere near the sanctuary. Perhaps it might form the basis of a renewed *porrectio instrumentorum* at ordination and commissioning rites.

I have a great deal of sympathy with those who are turned off by both these caricatures. They are not the whole story, of course, because education and liturgy do overlap, though they are distinct; and therapy and liturgy also overlap, but are in other ways different. The liturgy *is* the educational matrix of the church, and it is also the place where healing and spiritual growth can have their strongest focus. Each liturgical symbolism is more than what either of these facinating developments can carry. We are not meant to understand the liturgy, but we are meant to relate to it. We are not meant to gain psychological maturity through the liturgy, but we are meant to carry on in that fitful way which involves progress and regression in the rather messy manner known to the greatest Christian souls down the ages. I don't want to understand the full implications of the cross during one single perfect Good Friday liturgy; nor do I want to get rid of my hangups when faced with the paschal liturgy of light, at a single go. Education and growth are part of the liturgy, but to predetermine what is learned or to hasten how we are to grow inevitably means that the liturgy will snap, because it is approached by people whose expectations are too heavy and too specific.

Symbols and signs are utterly different, yet we often prefer that the liturgy were full of signs instead of symbols.[6] Signs are performative and reach a predetermined end; symbols express an intention and achieve their end at the same time. Signs manipulate; symbols do not because they resound and suggest. Signs do not express but perform; symbols do not perform but achieve what they signify. Signs do not communicate at the personal level; symbols communicate creatively at the personal level and are part of a real "encounter." All of this means that the

6. See David N. Power, *Unsearchable Riches: The Symbolic Nature of Liturgy* (New York: Pueblo, 1984).

symbols of Holy Week are not taken in at a glance, because they are meant to help us continue to relate to things, truths, realities which a signpost cannot convey. The driver of a car would not know what to do if faced with a road sign which had a cross on it; nor would the faithful on Palm Sunday if suddenly given a "No Entry" sign instead of a palm cross, and if a person were given that sign, it would be taken to suggest something else, and would baffle the pious and perhaps even amuse the tortuous.

We have had so much symbolism during these liturgical excursions into history. Wood and tree on Palm Sunday and Good Friday. Light and water at the Easter Vigil. Walking around in order to give a sense of corporate identity to the worshipers and continuity between the various "events." Plenty of time to reflect on the central narratives of the drama, the stories of the passion of Christ. All these are universal symbols, even including the oils used at the baptism liturgy, and the bread and wine of the eucharist. There is no need for us to be self-conscious about them, and yet many of us are. And the clergy do not help when they use symbolism minimalistically after long explanation, whereas what they ought to be doing is to use symbols lavishly after brief and imaginative explanation, if there is to be an explanation at all. There are such things as parish magazines and many other means whereby the curious, those who "like that sort of thing," to use the immortal words of Miss Jean Brodie, may glean some of the background information. But liturgy is not about information: it is about celebration. That essential difference passes beyond the understanding of many people today, right across the spectrum. If we were to be more natural in using these symbols, we would become more thoughtful, too, in the liturgy.[7]

All these observations could be applied to everyday liturgy, but they have a particular application to the Great

7. See John E. Burkhart, *Worship: A Searching Examination of the Liturgical Experience* (Philadelphia: Westminster, 1982) 23–27.

Week, which is focused on the Vigil, that ancient relic which probably goes right back to the time of the New Testament. The Pasch is the Christian Passover, and the name abounds in early literature to describe the annual celebration of the death and resurrection of Christ, the one single unitive liturgical event. Naturally, Christians took care to explain the relation between the new and the old. Preachers like Melito of Sardis (170) and Origen (d.253/4) delight in typology. Melito makes the connection in words such as these:

> O strange, inexplicable mystery! The sacrifice of a sheep is the salvation of Israel, and the death of a sheep becomes the life of the people, and his blood deters the angel.

Origen thinks of the sacrifice of Isaac when he writes:

> You see that to lose something for God is to get it back multiplied for yourself. The Gospels promise other things besides: a hundredfold is promised for you and also eternal life in Christ Jesus our Lord, to whom is glory and power forever and ever.[8]

The Paschal Liturgy

Origins

From an early time the Easter Vigil consisted of twelve Old Testament readings which ranged from creation, through covenant and redemption, and prophecy, to end with the eucharist. When baptism becomes closely linked with the vigil, which was probably sometime in the late second or early third century, the baptism came between the readings and the eucharist. And the whole service probably began with the lighting of the lamps, a custom which the early Christians borrowed from Jewish Sabbath

8. Translation by Thomas Halton in Hamman, *The Paschal Mystery* 29 (Melito, *De Pascha*) and 49 (Origen, *On Genesis 22:1–14, Homily* 8).

practice. So there you have in embryo: light, word, baptism, and eucharist.

Two distinct interpretations can be discerned in the Christian use of "Pascha."[9] The earliest is that of Pascha as *passio* ("passion"). Christ is the main protagonist. But as so often with a new idea, it is necessary to bring the community into the event. As early as 1 Corinthians 5:6–8 ("Christ our Passover is sacrificed for us") and John 13:1 ("Before the feast of Passover Jesus, knowing that his hour had come to pass from this world to the father . . . "), the second interpretation of Pascha is being developed: Pascha is a "passing," a "passage" in which the *Christian* is the protagonist. The implications of these two ideas result in the two emphases which have lived together down the ages. On the one hand you have Holy Week as "event"; and on the other you have Holy Week as "mystery in which the Christian grows." In the third century it is the second idea which takes over, and it proves grist to the mill of writers who want to link baptism almost exclusively with Easter, like Cyril of Jerusalem in the fourth century.

But for fixing the Pasch as a regular "date" for Christians, the New Testament is divided in its chronology. The synoptics make the Passover the day of the Last Supper, whereas John regards Friday as the day of Passover, the day of Christ's death. Some Christians in Asia Minor obstinately held to the Johannine chronology and celebrated the Pasch on every 14th Nisan, the day of the Jewish Passover, whereas the rest of the church celebrated it on the nearest Sunday. It was still a unitive festival, whether you were what scholars call a Quartodeciman and Johannine, or whether you went for the nearest Sunday because each Sunday is a day of the resurrection. Differences such as these threatened the unity of the church.[10] At first people like Pope Anicetus in Rome followed "the tradition of the

9. See Taft, "Historicism Revisited" 16ff.
10. Talley, *The Origins of the Liturgical Year* 1–27.

presbyters" and did what most people did, with Pasch on Sunday, whereas Polycarp in Smyrna took the tougher chronology of John, which was one of the reasons for his visit to Anicetus in Rome about 154. A few Quartodecimans lingered on in Asia Minor as late as the fifth century, long after the dispute was officially settled in the latter part of the second century. This is yet one more example of how rigorists (the Quartodecimans) give in to progressives (everyone else). It cannot be denied that it is more logical to keep the Pasch in the more Jewish manner. Irenaeus tells us that the Pasch began with an evening vigil in which everyone stood because of the importance of the occasion, and those who were baptized, if there were baptisms, fasted beforehand. Similar reflections are to be found in the writings of other theologians. Perhaps Augustine puts it best of all:

On this night all the world keeps vigil,
the hostile and the reconciled worlds.
The reconciled one does it to praise the Healer;
the hostile one to pour insult on the judge
who had passed the unfavourable verdict.
The one keeps vigil all vibrant and resplendent in
    tenderness;
the other's vigil is with trembling and gnashing of teeth.[11]

Augustine brings together the themes of vigil, fall and restoration, spiritual growth and conflict. This is the nub of the matter. The death and resurrection of Christ is the foundation of the Christian faith. It does not "start" at Christmas; it begins at the Pasch, because the Pasch holds together both the creatureliness of the Christian and the fact of the Christian as the redeemed and restored and reborn person, with an individuality which is affirmed by God.[12] When the disciples discerned the Lord in his resur-

11. Translation by Thomas Halton in Hamman, *The Paschal Mystery* 148 (Augustine, *Sermo* 219).
12. See, for example, the powerful discussion of this theme in J. Moltmann, *The Crucified God* (London: S.C.M., 1974) 291ff.

rection, they recognized an *individuality*, however that is to be understood and interpreted. So often we make Christ faceless and anonymous, largely because we make ourselves faceless and anonymous.

The Jerusalem liturgy at the time of Egeria's visit and Cyril's episcopate had the elements of lections, baptism, and eucharist, and was probably preceded by the lighting of the lamps, although to what extent the lamps were given any special Easter symbolism is in doubt.[13] The fifth century lectionary of Jerusalem implies that the candle was symbolic, held by the bishop and shared by all. Then, after twelve readings the baptism took place a midnight, and the whole liturgy had its climax in the eucharist. It cannot be emphasized just what effect this entire service had on those who were baptized, especially if it happened at Jerusalem. (Cyril's educational psychology in exactly what he explained *beforehand* to the candidates and what he explained *afterwards* would make a fascinating study. He takes great care in choosing his words.[14]) Above all, the liturgy of initiation was a unity, and it was part of the eucharist. It all seems so obvious and perhaps ideal in the way that it is described by those fourth century homilists, whether it is Cyril himself, or John Chrysostom, or Theodore of Mopsuestia, or Ambrose of Milan. They are all very different personalities, with different liturgies, different people, different environments with which to preach and celebrate.[15] But they are all at one in affirming the solidarity of Christian people with their Lord and with one

13. Wilkinson, *Egeria's Travels* 66–68. See also Robert F. Taft, *The Liturgy of the Hours in East and West: The Origins of the Divine Office and Its Meaning for Today* (Collegeville: The Liturgical Press, 1986), esp. 52ff.

14. See E. Yarnold, "Initiation: Sacrament and Experience" in Stevenson (ed.), *Liturgy Reshaped* 17–31.

15. See Hugh M. Riley, *Christian Initiation: A Comparative Study of the Interpretation of the Baptismal Liturgy in the Mystagogical Writings of Cyril of Alexandria, John Chrysostom, Theodore of Mopsuestia, and Ambrose of Milan*, Studies in Christian Antiquity 17 (Washington: Catholic University of America, 1974).

another in the two fundamental sacraments of the new covenant. Gregory Nazianzus in a passionate sermon preached in 362 gathers all this together:

> Yesterday I was crucified with Christ; today I will be glorified with him. Yesterday I died with Christ; today I will return to life with him. Yesterday I was buried with Christ; today I will rise with him from the tomb. Let us then carry our first-fruits to him who has suffered and risen for us . . . let us offer ourselves; it is the most precious and dearest gift in the eyes of God.[16]

Development

But the trouble is that the subsequent history of this united feast is a miserable tale of fragmentation, both in initiation and in the Easter celebration.[17] Initiation survives, but as a relic, in the later Middle Ages, for most baptisms were celebrated elsewhere in the liturgical year. And confirmation eventually becomes something which no one is sure about, except that the bishop is the only person who can do it. The vigil itself becomes anticipated. From as early as the eighth century in the West the celebration begins in the afternoon, with the result that the eucharist is an evening liturgy, not an early morning one. In the twelfth century the vigil starts at midday. Eventually it is anticipated to the extent of beginning early on Saturday morning, thus compounding the felony, destroying the chronology, ruining the symbolism by that common phenomenon in Christian liturgy known to all the churches, namely, expediency. No wonder that the Reformers swept aside this ancient service, and no wonder that Anglican and Lutheran books simply provide collect and readings for a eucharist on Easter morning, corre-

---

16. Translation by Thomas Halton in Hamman, *The Paschal Mystery* 76 (Gregory of Nazianzus, *Sermo I: On Easter*, 3).
17. On the timing of this liturgy, see Schmidt, *Hebdomada Sancta* II 873ff.

sponding with the Easter morning Mass which had grown up during the time when the vigil was being anticipated. In 1951 special permission was given in the Roman Catholic Church to hold the vigil late at night.[18] Because baptism would probably only take place at this service in exceptional circumstances and in order to identify the faithful with the baptismal character of the vigil eucharist, a new feature of the liturgy was introduced, the renewal of baptismal vows. Then, in 1956, a full revision of all the Holy Week services was made, which paved the way for the more thoroughgoing revision after the Second Vatican Council. Anglicans have followed suit in various ways appropriate to the circumstances. The best example of this is in the 1979 Book of Common Prayer of the American Episcopal Church, in which the Roman methods are followed; American Lutherans adopt this adaptation.[19] It tends to be less fussy and more flexible. Thus, the vigil can be considered simplified to suit local needs; but if the vigil is not held, some of the ceremonies of the light can be prefixed to the main Easter morning eucharist. This has the advantage of enriching a festal morning eucharist, and it also recognizes that for most Christians Easter is a "morning" affair. Some parishes experiment with liturgies at dawn, followed by a breakfast. Others anticipate the vigil earlier into nightfall on Saturday, rather than base it around midnight. Again others hold the vigil at night, and then adjourn until early morning. The number of options is great. But the danger with options is that basic principles can be ignored. Their advantage is that imaginative minds can adapt the historic liturgy to local requirements and traditions.

18. See a chronicle made after the sporadic reintroduction of this liturgy in France, J. Heintz, "La célébration de la vigile pascale en France," *La Maison-Dieu* 37 (1954) 121–124.

19. See *The Book of Common Prayer* 283–295; *Lutheran Book of Worship* (Minister's Desk Edition) 143–153. See also (Canadian Anglican) *Book of Alternative Services* (Toronto: Anglican Book Centre, 1985) 322–332.

Ceremonies of Light

The vigil begins with the *liturgy of light*.[20] Traditionally this comes in three parts: the blessing of the fire and lighting of the candle; the procession; and the paschal proclamation. The blessing of the fire is probably the oldest of all, whose ancestor is the blessing of lamps at the ancient Christian vespers, a custom still observed by Byzantine rite Christians. Placing grains of incense in the paschal candle is a custom sanctified by the cult of the wounds of Christ, but is probably based on a misinterpretation of an older practice of blessing the paschal candle with a lighted taper, *faciens crucem de incenso,* namely, "making a cross with a lighted (taper)."[21] The old French rite before the time of Charlemagne liked to light the paschal candle from a special taper which was kept from the end of the Maundy Thursday Mass.

Then the paschal candle is carried solemnly in procession into the church, with the threefold cry of "The Light of Christ" and the sharing of the light among the congregation.[22] This was originally intended to be as dramatic as possible. The old Roman rite (conservative to its back teeth) avoided the French and Spanish innovation of a single, large Easter candle, and at first processed with two candles, which were placed on either side of the pope for the liturgy of the word, on either side of the font for the baptism, and on either side of the altar for the eucharist. In Spain the paschal candle was brought suddenly in a blaze of light from the sacristy so that the effect is quite different from the gradual procession into the church. This

20. See Kenneth Stevenson, "The Ceremonies of Light—Their Shape and Function in the Paschal Vigil Liturgy," *Ephemerides Liturgicae* 99 (1985) 170–185.
21. See Bernard Capelle, "Le rite des cinq grains d'encens" in *Travaux Liturgiques* III 221–234. See also Schmidt, *Hebdomada Sancta* II 809–826.
22. See Bernard Capelle, "La procession du Lumen Christi au Samedi Saint" in *Travaux Liturgiques* III 221–234. See also Schmidt, *Hebdomada Sancta* II 809–826.

Spanish procedure resembles the Jerusalem Byzantine practice where the light is taken dramatically from the tomb where Christ is "buried."

The old way of blessing the paschal candle was simply a prayer, with the sign of the cross. The West developed its own form, in the proclamation known by the opening word of the standard Latin text, Exultet ("Rejoice").[23] Hymns to light are common. The oldest hymn of this kind which we know of is the *phos hilaron*—"Hail, gladdening light," which is still sung at the beginning of solemn vespers in the Byzantine rite. The fourth century Latin hymn "Inventor rutuli" by Prudentius is similarly based on the theme of light, and was sometimes used in the later Middle Ages during the procession of the candle into the church. But to sing a special hymn over the Easter light is something different. Jerome, in a letter to Praesidius in 334, refers to the practice in Piacenza of the deacon proclaiming a "candle-song." Ennodius, who was bishop of Pavia from 517–521, is supposed to have composed the two alternative "blessings of the candle" which bear his name, each of which begins in the preface form, *Vere dignum*. In Spain in 633, the Fourth Council of Toledo lays down that the lamp *and* the candle must both be blessed, presumably because the lamp lights the candle, and perhaps because the candle is so big that it must be lit in a special manner. Various texts appear in the old books, some longer than others, and some include the preface-opening with the "Lift up your hearts" dialogue. It is only in the Gothic Missal, an old seventh century book, that the Exultet first appears as an opening. The 1970 Missal provides both a short and a long version, which have influenced other modern texts including the British Joint Liturgical Group (1971, 1983), the American Episcopal (1979), and the Church of England (1986). Its opening speaks for itself:

23. See Schmidt, *Hebdomada Sancta* II 627–663 for texts, sources, and notes.

Rejoice, heavenly powers! Sing, choirs of angels!
Exult, all creation around God's throne!
Jesus Christ, our King, is risen!
Sound the trumpet of salvation!

Rejoice, O earth, in shining splendour,
radiant in the brightness of your King!
Christ has conquered! Glory fills you!
Darkness vanishes for ever!

Rejoice, O Mother Church! Exult in glory!
The risen Saviour shines upon you!
Let this place resound with joy,
echoing the mighty song of all God's people.[24]

Heaven, earth, and the people of God unite to sing the glories of him who has called us out of darkness into his own marvelous light. How appropriate that this hymn should be sung by a deacon, whose ministry of *diaconia* ("service") focuses on the secret of Christ's life, teaching, and example, whether or not he is able to sing some of the elaborate chants which have come down to us!

The 1970 Missal provides options in this first part of the paschal liturgy.[25] The service begins with a short introduction, which leads into a simple blessing of the source of light, the taper (called the "new fire"). Then the paschal candle *may* be marked with Alpha and Omega and the calendar year, together with the alleged "incense grains," although these later medieval ceremonies may be omitted. The candle is then brought into the church, to the strains of the threefold cry *Lumen Christi* ("Christ our Light") during which everyone's candles are gradually lit. The paschal candle is then placed on its stand, preferably next to the lectern, since that makes a fundamental statement

24. *The Sacramentary* 175; *Holy Week Services by the Joint Liturgical Group* (1971) 38; *Holy Week Services—The Joint Liturgical Group* (1983) 85; (American Episcopal) *Book of Common Prayer* 286; *Lent Holy Week Easter: Services and Prayers* 230.
25. *The Sacramentary* 170ff.

about divine illumination and the word of God, which is what the vigil is all about. The Exultet follows, in either version, though there is scope for countries to compose their own. The texts provided are abbreviations of the later medieval versions. While the *laus apium* ("praise of bees") has been suppressed, the section referring to the *felix culpa* ("happy fault") appears only in the longer version. This part of the Exultet proved controversial in the Middle Ages. Hugh of Cluny had it expunged from the Cluniac versions, and some countries followed suit; for example, extant Danish and German books leave it out, whereas Swedish books leave it in.[26] The chant has long fascinated musicians, as well as those deacons fortunate (or unfortunate) enough to have to sing it! Originally it was sung to a chant like the eucharistic prayer, but soon the music elaborated. Two versions were popular in the Middle Ages, one Norman, the other Beneventan, but the former replaced the latter from the thirteenth century, when the Norman conquest of Italy reached the center of the country.[27]

The Exultet has been called *laus cerei* ("praise of the candle) as well as *praeconium paschale* ("paschal proclamation"). It certainly reads like a Christian form of the Jewish Passover Haggadah, the joyous explanation of the meaning of the Passover; and it may well be derived from such a source. However, it should be noted that, whereas western rites elaborate their light ceremonies through various means, including the special paschal candle and sharing the light in a large building, the eastern rites keep to a simpler form, avoiding the special candle and using

26. See Schmidt, *Hebdomada Sancta* II 644ff. See also Strömberg, *The Manual from Bystrop* 39ff.
27. Schmidt, *Hebdomada Sancta* II 948ff.

prayers which emphasize spiritual illumination as an epiphany of God's redemption.[28]

The Word

The 1970 Missal adheres to the traditional order, which moves from the ceremonies of light to the vigil readings and eucharistic synaxis. However, in 1971 the British Joint Group issued its first Holy Week book which contained a vigil rite which *began* with the lections and moved into the ceremonies of light as the consummation of that watching and waiting. The 1983 services of this Group followed suit, partly because by 1971 there were Roman Catholic members on the Joint Liturgical Group, and partly perhaps because the new shape had commended itself to many people. Roman Catholics in Britain began, from 1979, to experiment with this shape.[29]

The argument put forward for this new shape was that the vigil readings should happen in a darkened church so that the liturgy could move from darkness to light. Dissat-

28. See Stevenson, "The Ceremonies of Light," esp. 179ff. Compare Robert F. Taft, "'Thanksgiving for the Light'. Towards a Theology of Vespers" in *Beyond East and West* 127–149. There seems to be a fundamental weakness in many of the modern liturgies at this point, especially when the building concerned is a large one, and the threefold cry of *Lumen Christi* does not have sufficient impact. An alternative practice, which adapts the medieval tradition of singing a hymn at this juncture, would be to use the hymn "Through the night of doubt and sorrow" as a processional. (The hymn is a translation by Baring-Gould of the Danish hymn by Bernard Ingemann, "Igjennem nat og traengsel"; see Frost, *Historical Companion to Hymns Ancient and Modern* 301.) But it should be sung as four, not eight, stanzas, even halting between the verses and singing *Lumen Christi*. Words, music, and context match well.

29. *Holy Week Services by the Joint Liturgical Group* (1971) 34ff.; *Holy Week Services—The Joint Liturgical Group* (1983) 76ff. This matter is discussed in detail in Stevenson, "Ceremonies of Light" 171ff. (and chart, 184). The Roman Catholic text which follows this structure is to be found in *Lord, By Your Cross and Resurrection: Celebrating Holy Week* (Westminster: St. Thomas More Centre for Pastoral Liturgy, 1979).

isfaction was expressed with the traditional Roman Catholic order in which the symbolism of light seemed to go all at once, so that the atmosphere of watching and waiting could not persist; all was revealed too soon, on this reckoning. When the Church of England came to authorize its own official services, it took a middle line, not for the sake of an Anglican compromise (!), but after carefully reading the history of the Paschal Vigil in the East, where the vesper candle ceremonies still constitute an important part of solemn vespers in the Byzantine rite. With a background such as this, what happens to the special Easter light? The answer to this question comes from the tenth century Jerusalem rite which has been studied in detail by Bertonière. Here the sequence of rites is as follows:

vespers of the burial of Christ;
phos hilaron ("Hail, gladdening light"), the vesper candle hymn;
vigil readings;
the light: shared from the tomb of Christ by all;
end of vespers;
baptisms;
eucharist.[30]

Such a scheme has the advantage of building up to the revelation of the resurrection of Christ so that the vesper light matches the vigil readings, and the Easter light is near the Easter gospel. The 1986 Church of England rite, while allowing the Roman Catholic structure to be followed, takes the view that this old Jerusalem shape is better, and it goes so far as to recommend that the gospel be read before the Exultet.[31] Whether or not this adaptation of eastern symbolism catches on remains to be seen. It is surely complex and runs against the grain of previous western tradition. Moreover, rhythm is of paramount im-

30. See G. Bertonière, *The Historical Development of the Easter Vigil and Related Services in the Greek Church*, Orientalia Christiana Analecta 193 (Rome: Pontificium Institutum Orientalium Studiorum, 1972).
31. *Lent Holy Week Easter: Services and Prayers* 223ff.

portance on special occasions, since special liturgies will never become digested by the faithful unless they have a standard format and allow themselves to be repeated again and again, year after year. Nonetheless, such a scheme continues the western story of adaptation and synthesis, and it also shows up the poverty of many modern services (in which we can only read the word at one "go"), by dividing the vigil readings from the eucharistic ones. By making such a claim, we are alerted to the different character of the two sets of lections, which is a timely move.

In the 1970 Missal the readings themselves have been reduced to a more manageable length from the old twelve: in 1956 they were reduced to four; in 1970 they went up to eight, but these are not all necessary.[32] They lead straight into the eucharistic synaxis, and each lection is followed by a chant and suitable collect. The themes are similar to the old ones: Genesis 1:1–2:2 (creation), Genesis 22:1–18 (Abraham's sacrifice), Exodus 14:15–15:1 (through the Red Sea), Isaiah 54:5–14 (the Redeemer's mercy), Isaiah 55:1–11 ("come to the water"), Baruch 3:9–15,32–4:4 ("turn back and seize the Law"), Ezekiel 36:16–28 ("clean water"), and Romans 6:3–11 ("dying and rising with Christ"). Some of these readings are a bit obscure; they can of course be altered. The American Episcopal and Lutheran books are simpler and include Ezekiel 37:1–14 (the valley of the dry bones).[33] The singing of the *Gloria* is usually greeted with bell-ringing and any musical instrument that is available, suitable, and played well.

32. See Schmidt, *Hebdomada Sancta* II 827ff. and *Hebdomada Sancta* I 138ff. See also *The Sacramentary* 187ff., *Ordo Lectionum Missae* 26ff.
33. *Lutheran Book of Worship* (Minister's Desk Edition) 149. *Book of Common Prayer* 291.

Baptism

After word, we move to baptism. The old western rites were complex, not least in the blessing of the water.[34] A litany sometimes fills in the time that it takes to process from the place of the word to that of baptism. This works well, especially when the refrain is easy to pick up, and when the litany includes prayer for those about to be baptized, or else for the baptismal growth of the community. The blessing of water in the 1970 Missal is an abbreviation of the old, and much of it dates back to the old Gelasian Sacramentary which, at this point, is sixth century Roman. The blessing of water in the American Prayer Book is a fine composition, drafted by Leonel Mitchell, and based on various sources.

We thank you, Almighty God, for the gift of water.
Over it the Holy Spirit moved in the beginning of creation.
Through it you led the children of Israel out of their bond-
  age into Egypt into the land of promise.
In it your Son Jesus received the baptism of John
  and was anointed by the Holy Spirit as the Messiah, the
Christ,
  to lead us, through his death and resurrection,
  from the bondage of sin into everlasting life.
We thank you, Father, for the water of Baptism.
In it we are buried with Christ in his death.
By it we share in his resurrection.
Through it we are reborn by the Holy Spirit.
Therefore in joyful obedience, we bring into his fellowship
  those who come to him in faith, baptizing them
  in the Name of the Father, and of the Son, and of the
  Holy Spirit.

34. Schmidt, *Hebdomada Sancta* II 847ff. See also Leonel L. Mitchell, "The Thanksgiving over the Water in the Baptismal Rite of the Western Church" in B. D. Spinks (ed.), *The Sacrifice of Praise: Studies in the Themes of Thanksgiving and Redemption in the Central Prayers of the Eucharistic and Baptismal Liturgies*, Bibliotheca Ephemerides Liturgicae "Subsidia" 19 (Rome: Edizioni Liturgiche, 1981) 229–244.

Now sanctify this water, we pray you, by the power of
your Holy Spirit,
that those who here are cleansed from sin and born again
may continue for ever in the risen life of Jesus Christ
our Saviour.[35]

Originally this great blessing of water (rightly called
"the baptismal prayer" in those churches which still fear
objective blessing of water!) sufficed for all the baptisms
in the year to come, since it was felt that any baptisms
other than those which took place on Easter night were
in a real sense derivative. It is, therefore, hard for us to
grasp the impact of this prayer and the accompaning baptismal liturgy unless there is a baptism. For even if the
faithful merely "renew baptismal promises," a 1951 innovation to give the restored vigil a baptismal character,[36]
they cannot enter into the baptismal mystery in nearly
such a powerful manner as they can when baptism is celebrated in this fundamentally baptismal feast. The American Episcopal Book (1979) tries to give some emphasis to
the moral and social demands of baptism by including
these aspects in the baptismal vows.[37] Such a variation on
an ancient theme may be right and worthy, but it is second
best to the Christian community celebrating the sacraments together at Easter.

Eucharist

The eucharist comes as the climax of the whole night,
indeed of the whole Great Week and Lent. While some
churches may "phase" the liturgy so that it lasts through
the hours of Saturday evening and Sunday morning, others may adjourn the vigil so that the baptism and eucharist

35. *Book of Common Prayer* 306ff.; see Hatchett, *Commentary on the American Prayer Book* 274ff.
36. H. Jenny, "Pourquoi renouveler les engagements du baptême dans la nuit de pâques?," *La Maison-Dieu* 28 (1952) 63–79.
37. *Book of Common Prayer* 304ff.

are celebrated at midnight or, better still, dawn. These are practical matters which will vary from place to place. What is *not* desirable is that the whole service is so domesticated that it all happens in the early evening of Saturday, and no impression is given that it is toilsome, awkward, and hard. But however it is celebrated, the words of the post-communion prayer ring bells at once ancient and startingly contemporary when it prays:

> Lord, you have nourished us with your Easter sacraments.
> Fill us with the Spirit of your love
> and make us all one in heart.[38]

Here survives—in spite of history, controversy, and all the fuss of "Churchianity"—the deeply traditional and deeply Christian way of holding death and resurrection, light and word, baptism and eucharist—together.

---

38. *The Sacramentary* 206. For sources, see Chapter Three, note 36.

CHAPTER SIX

EPILOGUE: EVERY EUCHARIST IS EASTER

Almighty God, the Father, who raised up His Son from the dead, by the power of the Holy Ghost; Quicken you from the death of sin unto the life of righteousness; and pour out abundantly upon you the Spirit of adoption.

The Lord Jesus Christ, the Resurrection and the Life, who as on this day took again His body from the grave, bringing life and immortality to light; Shine into your hearts in the glory of His Spirit, and give unto you, by the same Spirit, the knowledge of the Father and of the Son.

The Holy Ghost, the Spirit of the Father and of the Son, who quickeneth the dead, and by whom we are all baptized into the Body of Christ; Vouchsafe unto you the increase of spiritual life and health; and shed abroad in your hearts the love of God, that ye may rejoice in the hope of His glory.[1]

THE NINETEENTH CENTURY produced many religious movements in all the mainstream churches. One group which began in the 1830s was later called "Catholic Apostolic." It soon adopted a rich liturgy, which can with some credibility be regarded as the first ecumenical service

---

1. *Liturgy and Other Divine Offices of the Church* (London: Pitman, 1880) 222.

book.[2] In their eucharistic liturgy a solemn blessing was given before communion on special occasions, and the one quoted in full above appears for use on Easter day.

The origin of this prayer is the same as the seasonal blessings which appear in the 1970 Missal, but which are given at the *end* of Mass, namely in the practice of the old Spanish ("Visigothic") and French ("Gallican") churches to have an episcopal blessing before communion for the benefit of those not staying to partake of the eucharist.[3] Thus the compilers of the 1970 Missal and of the 1851 edition of the Catholic Apostolic Liturgy followed the old sources, but each adapted them in a particular way.[4]

This Easter blessing is lengthy, rich, vibrant, redolent of many themes, and aggressively Trinitarian in its theology.[5] But one underlying theme holds these many ideas together, and that is *theophany*. The prayer is a solemn affirmation of God's presence in the liturgy in general, and at this Easter communion in particular. The language is evocative and resonant, but this does not obscure the one essential thing that is needful, namely, that the faithful are ready in heart and mind to grow in the Easter faith through righteousness, knowledge of heavenly things, and the spiritual life.

We have travelled far and wide, through many countries and centuries, and although our primary concern has

2. Kenneth Stevenson, "The Catholic Apostolic Church—Its History and Its Eucharist," *Studia Liturgica* 13 (1979) 21–45, and "The Liturgical Year in the Catholic Apostolic Church," *Studia Liturgica* 14 (1982) 128–134. See also David H. Tripp, "The Liturgy of the Catholic Apostolic Church," *Scottish Journal of Theology* 22 (1969) 437–454.

3. See E. E. Moeller, *Corpus Benedictionum Pontificalium*, Corpus Christianorum, series latina, CLXII (Turnholti: Brepols, 1971).

4. See E. E. Moeller, "Les bénédictions solennelles du nouveau missel romain," *Questions Liturgiques* 271 (1971) 317–325, and Kenneth Stevenson, "The Catholic Apostolic Eucharist," Southampton University Ph.D. Dissertation, 1975, 191–195.

5. This is a feature of the liturgy of this church. See Stevenson, Dissertation, 324ff.

been to illuminate the Holy Week rites of the 1970 Missal, we have taken in many other liturgies. And this obscure and neglected nineteenth century liturgy provides us with a high note on which to conclude, because it is at the conclusion of our reflections on this great mystery of salvation that we should be recalled to fundamentals. Above all, Easter liturgy is a sacrament of *encounter* between Christ and the faithful. This is why symbolism, verbal as well as non-verbal, is so important, because when we are dealing with cross and rising, we are indeed dealing with the inexpressible.

The whole message of the Great Week, however, is that these inexpressible "events" which lie at the heart of the various liturgies are mysteries which are celebrated and brought before God for our own good, that we "may rejoice in the hope of His glory," as the Catholic Apostolic blessing says at the end. Perhaps because of the centrality of Easter to the Christian faith, there has long persisted a tradition that affirms that every Sunday is Easter day since Sunday is the Day of the Resurrection. One late fourth century bishop, Severian of Gabala, goes even further and insists that every *eucharist* is Easter:

> Is there not a Passover of the Church every Sunday?
> Surely some new victim is not offered in that feast?
> Surely the Passover is not one immolation and the eucharist another?
> Surely there is not one beautiful mystery in the Passover, and then another one on Sunday, and Wednesday and Friday?
> For as often as you make the memorial of the passion of Christ, you make Passover![6]

---

6. Quoted by Frans Van De Paverd, *Zur Geschichte des Messliturgie in Antiocheia und Konstantinopel gegen Ende des Vierten Jahrtausends: Analyse der Quellen bei Johannes Chrysostomos*, Orientalia Christiana Analecta 187 (Rome: Pontificium Institutum Orientalium Studiorum, 1979) 66 n.2. Text in J. B. Aucher, *Severiani sive Seberiani Gabalorum Episcopi Emesensis Homiliae* (Venetiis, 1827) 187; from Homily 5.

Severian's hearers would have picked up the allusion to the Pauline command to repeat the eucharist (1 Cor 11:26). This preacher's dogged determination to spread Easter over the whole Christian experience was no doubt aimed at those who went overboard with "historicism" as a convenient means of locking God up in neat and manageable compartments.

We meet the same kind of insistence in the Danish Lutheran tradition of hymn writing. Thomas Kingo, bishop of Odense in the seventeenth century, was one of the great founders of such a native tradition. High Lutheran in theology, he was eloquently succeeded in the eighteenth century by the Pietist, Hans Brorson, bishop of Ribe. But in many ways this tradition reaches its peak in the nineteenth century through the writings of Nikolai Grundtvig, whom we mentioned in the previous chapter in relation to his use of natural imagery at Easter. For Grundtvig, Easter, baptism and eucharist, preaching and congregation, bell ringing and hymn singing, all meet in a joyous statement of God's grace in the risen Christ.

> We are God's house of living stones,
> Builded for His habitation;
> He through baptismal grace us owns,
> Heirs of His wondrous salvation;
> Were we but two His name to tell,
> Yet, He would deign with us to dwell,
> With all His grace and His favour.
>
> Here stands the font before our eyes,
> Telling how God did receive us;
> Th'altar recalls Christ's sacrifice
> And what his table doth give us;
> Here sounds the word that doth proclaim
> Christ yesterday, today the same,
> Yea, and for aye our Redeemer.
>
> Grant then, O God, where'er men roam,
> That when the church bells are ringing,

98

Many in Jesus' faith may come
Where He His message is bringing:
I know mine own, mine own know me,
Ye, not the world, my face shall see:
My peace I leave with you. Amen.[7]

Many nuances are lost in the translation—the last line is in fact a direct quotation of the formula for the peace at communion—but that is the risk that is inherent when the liturgy migrates or borrows or adapts. And as old ideas are taken over by others, new ideas and insights are born. For all the mess we make of divine truths in our liturgies, we can at least take comfort in the fact that worshiping God is the most natural instinct he has given us.

Easter lives on, but we still live in Lent. The promise has been given, and the light shines in the darkness. We are a people chosen by God as vehicles of grace that is immeasurable. The Easter gospel, therefore, with its various themes of appearance, empty tomb, baptism and eucharist, does not beckon us to prove facts from which we can hit others so much as to grow in that grace which is sufficient for all that lies ahead.

So I return to Jerusalem, to the Sunday morning which I spent there during Lent in 1982. My father and I started off in the Church of the Holy Sepulcher, where no fewer than four eucharists were celebrated. The Coptic liturgy was well under way, at a small altar behind the Tomb. The anaphora they used was that of Basil of Caesarea, in the earlier "Alexandrian" version, which forms the basis of the American ecumenical "Common Eucharistic Prayer,"

7. English translation of "Kirken den er et gammel hus," *Den Danske Salmebog* no. 280.

as well as the fourth eucharistic prayer of the 1970 Missal.[8] But here it was to be found in its own milieu. Meanwhile, the Greek Orthodox were piping up in the "Catholicon" in the main part of the church, and their patriarch was about to preside at a grand celebration, in the course of which the longer "Byzantine" anaphora of Basil was used. The Syrian Orthodox, on the other hand, began their eucharist in a side-chapel, tucked away behind some columns. In that small and intimate atmosphere an Arab gathering met to celebrate the native Jerusalem liturgy of St. James in the native tongue of Jesus himself—Aramaic. Finally, the Roman Catholic community entered, somewhat Italianate in aspect and clothing, led by their archbishop, who presided in silk and ermine from a throne at a rather old-fashioned-looking Mass, at which the preacher was, appropriately, a Franciscan. The Greek liturgy ended with a procession round the Tomb, the patriarch carrying a relic of the cross, and preceded by deacons walking backwards and incensing the relic lavishly with pungent incense. I can still picture the faces of the people in these four congregations, although the Roman Catholics and Greek Orthodox (for all their impressive array of vestments) felt like onlookers too. The Copts earned their place in the antiquity of their liturgy and spirituality. But it is the little Syrian community that remains most vividly in my mind, in particular the simple gestures of their priest, all of which seemed to go right back, as it were, to the roots of it all.

Then we left them all to finish, and we took a short walk outside, round the corner, and found ourselves, by acci-

8. "Common Eucharistic Prayer" in, e.g., *Book of Common Prayer* 372ff. and *At the Lord's Table*, Supplemental Worship Resources 9 (Nashville: Abingdon, 1981) 22ff. Roman Catholic text in *The Sacramentary* 556ff. See also Leonel L. Mitchell, "The Alexandrian Anaphora of St. Basil of Caesarea: Ancient Source of 'A Common Eucharistic Prayer'," *Anglican Theological Review* 58 (1976) 194–206. See discussion of these texts in Kenneth Stevenson, *Eucharist and Offering* (New York: Pueblo, 1986) 201–203, 208, 210.

dent rather than design, in the German Lutheran Church of the Redeemer. We were suddenly back in western Christianity, sitting in serried ranks, a fine organ in the west gallery leading the hymns, and preceding each of them with the rendition of a short chorale prelude, which suggested the melody and at the same time offered an opportunity for the display of musical talent.

The theme of the service came from the lectionary, "Rejoice, Jerusalem!," both touching and trying for Germans to sing in Israel. We sang a metrical version of Psalm 84, "Wie lieblich schön, Herr Zebaoth, ist deine Vohnung, O mein Gott," and Johann Lindemann's hymn of joy, "In dir ist Freude,"[9] immortalized by Bach in a vivacious organ chorale prelude, which has a repeated pedal-run that undergirds the entire delightful piece. The sermon was a demanding twenty minutes of well thought-out and closely-argued spirituality, dwelling on the promise of redemption and the tensions with which the Christian has to live. At the communion, distributed to us in two enormous circles in the apse, pitta-bread and Mount Carmel wine made up the elements, consumed by each one of us. To cap it all, there was a baptism, at a font in a side aisle, which was decorated with local seasonal flowers. So we moved from our seats to witness the baptism, and to go up to the altar of God. Bang on midday, the concluding organ voluntary ended, and we walked out, with the rest of that international congregation.

But midday is a Moslem prayer-time, and from the minarettes came forth the chanted call to prayer. We were back in Jerusalem, the city claimed by three major faiths as holy and sacred. We were back in the Middle East. There's a parable in that somewhere, and I think it's called "after the vision—the task."

Heavenly Father,
you have delivered us from the power of darkness,

9. *Evangelische Kirchengesangbuch* (Göttingen: Vandenhoeck and Ruprecht, no date) 552ff.; the two hymns are nos. 184 and 288.

and brought us into the kingdom of your Son:
grant that, as his death has recalled us to life,
so his continual presence in us
may raise us to eternal joy. Amen.[10]

10. *Lent Holy Week Easter: Services and Prayers* 239. Text abbreviated
from the version in David Silk, *Prayers for Use at the Alternative Services*
(London: Mowbrays, 1980) 71, itself an updated version of the traditional English text given in William Bright, *Ancient Collects* (London:
Parker, 1875) 58. The original Latin text appears in the *Missale Mixtum*,
Migne, *Patrologia Latina* 86, col. 635, for the offices of matins and vespers on the Friday after Easter.

SELECT BIBLIOGRAPHY

Berger, Ruper, and Hans Hollerweger. *Celebrating the Easter Vigil.* New York: Pueblo, 1983.

Crichton, J. D. *The Liturgy of Holy Week.* Dublin: Veritas, 1983.

Hamman, A. *The Paschal Mystery.* Ancient Liturgies and Patristic Texts. Staten Island: Alba House, 1969.

Hardison, O. B., Jr. *Christian Rite and Christian Drama in the Middle Ages.* Baltimore: Johns Hopkins Press, 1969.

Martimort, A. G., ed. *The Church at Prayer: An Introduction to the Liturgy.* Vol. IV. *The Liturgy and Time.* Collegeville: The Liturgical Press, 1986.

Perham, Michael, and Kenneth Stevenson. *Waiting for the Risen Christ.* London: S.P.C.K., 1986.

Power, David N. *Unsearchable Riches: The Symbolic Nature of Liturgy.* New York: Pueblo, 1984.

Ruedi-Weber, Hans. *On a Friday Noon—Meditations on the Cross.* London: S.P.C.K., 1979.

Schmidt, Hermann. *Hebdomada Sancta* I and II. Rome: Herder, 1956, 1957.

Stevenson, Kenneth. "The Ceremonies of Light—Their Shape and Function in the Paschal Vigil Liturgy." *Ephemerides Liturgicae* 99 (1985) 170–185.

Stevenson, Kenneth. "On Keeping Holy Week." *Theology* 89 (1986) 32–38.

Taft, Robert F. *Beyond East and West: Problems in Liturgical Understanding.* Washington: The Pastoral Press, 1984.

Talley, Thomas J. *The Origins of the Liturgical Year.* New York: Pueblo, 1986.

Tyrer, John W. *Historical Survey of Holy Week, Its Services and Ceremonial.* Alcuin Club Collections 29. London: Milford, 1932.

Wilkinson, John. *Egeria's Travels.* 1st ed. London: S.P.C.K., 1971. 2nd ed. Jerusalem/Warminster: Ariel, 1981.

Williams, Rowan. *Resurrection.* London: Darton, Longman, and Todd, 1982.